CHESAPEAKE CITY

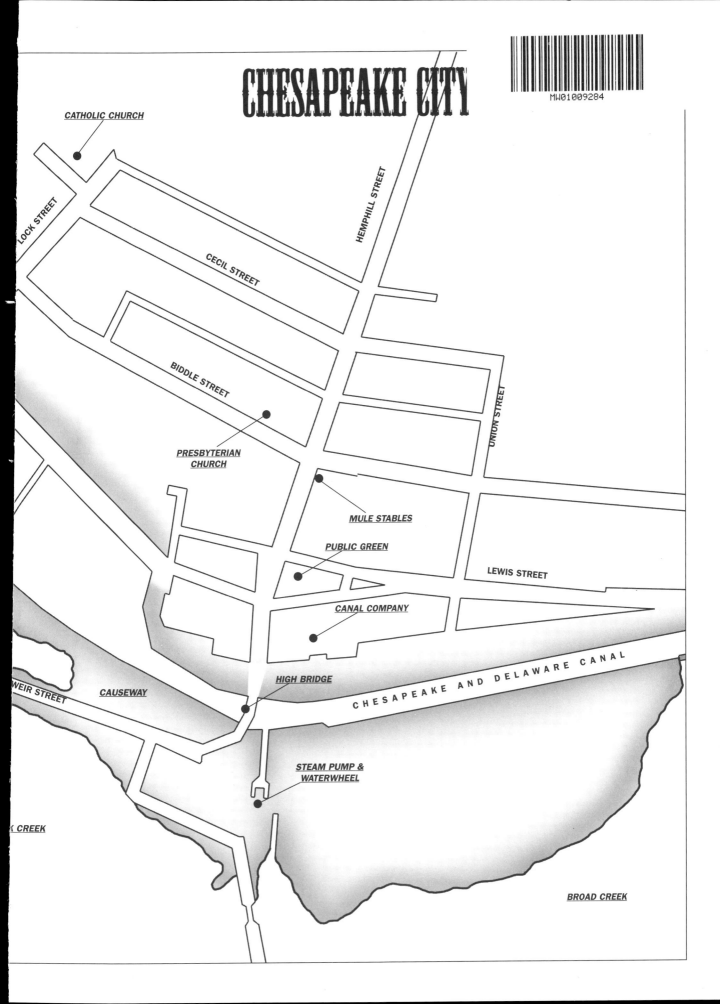

CATHOLIC CHURCH

LOCK STREET

HEMPHILL STREET

CECIL STREET

BIDDLE STREET

UNION STREET

PRESBYTERIAN
CHURCH

MULE STABLES

PUBLIC GREEN

LEWIS STREET

CANAL COMPANY

WEIR STREET

CAUSEWAY

HIGH BRIDGE

CHESAPEAKE AND DELAWARE CANAL

STEAM PUMP &
WATERWHEEL

CREEK

BROAD CREEK

10/30/15

Natalie,

Wishing you many hours
of enjoyable reading!

Karen Morgan

CHESAPEAKE CITY

The Canal Town Through The Years

LONG BRIDGE, CHESAPEAKE CITY, MD.

Karen T. Morgan and J. Kevin Titter

Briscoe Hill Publishers
Chesapeake City, MD

Copyright 2000 by
Briscoe Hill Publishers
Chesapeake City, Maryland

Second Edition, May 2001

Printed in USA
by
Thomson-Shore, Inc.
Dexter, Michigan

Layout & Design
by
J. Kevin Titter

Editors
C. M. Krause and S. M. Young

Library of Congress control number: 00-091921
ISBN: 0-9703918-0-3

Dedication

To our families, who spent countless hours helping,
encouraging, hoping, and waiting –

Thanks for your patience.

To those who generously shared
their histories, reminiscing and recalling,
sorting and searching, in the effort to help
make this work as accurate as possible –

Thanks for the memories.

The Authors

Contents

Illustrations

Drawings by J. Kevin Titter

Drawing by Aaron P. Titter

WELCOME
TO
CHESAPEAKE CITY
SLOW DOWN

The earliest memories of Chesapeake City's oldest residents span the years 1915-1930. Those years are the highlight of this volume.

Along with documented history and facts,
we share the stories and remembrances of life in
this time, both engaging and bittersweet.

Gone is a simpler time – a more leisurely way of
living, even in the midst of hard work.
But the spirit and rural character of small-town
America survives in Chesapeake City.

We invite you to travel through these pages
to Chesapeake City as it once was.
Become captivated as you delve
into its rich, rural heritage.

"Welcome to Chesapeake City...
...Slow Down."

A
Brief
History

Chesapeake City Lock

Canal Workers, 1930

In 1829, the small wharf area of Bohemia Village on the banks of Back Creek was about to experience explosive growth. The story of this isolated area, located in the northeastern corner of Maryland, begins much earlier.

In the late 1600s, when there was no canal and no town of Chesapeake City, entrepreneurs dreamed of a commercial waterway to connect Chesapeake Bay and Delaware Bay. Augustine Herman, a surveyor for Lord Baltimore, first proposed the idea. Herman owned fifteen thousand acres on the northern Delmarva Peninsula, a property he named Bohemia Manor. Much of the land produced lumber

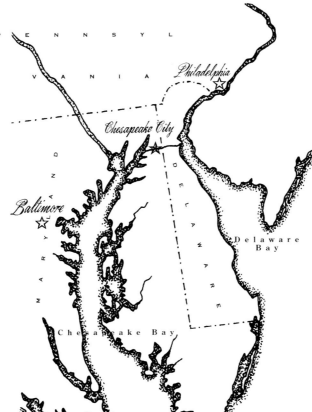

and farm crops which were laboriously hauled overland across the peninsula to the bays for further transport by water.

For one hundred years, plans for a canal were conceived and discarded. In 1804, a route was chosen for a canal which would connect the Christiana River, in Delaware, with the Elk River at a point near Frenchtown. Work began on the first phase of the project – a feeder canal to supply water from Big Elk Creek. The project was abandoned just two years later due to lack of funding. It was twenty-four years before canal construction resumed.

John Randal, Jr., a surveyor on the Erie Canal project, advocated a new route which would cut through three creeks in the northern part of the peninsula. In anticipation of its approval, Randal bought several hundred acres near the mouth of Back Creek, believing the area would develop into a busy port. In the years 1824 to 1829, the waterway became a reality with the construction of the Chesapeake and Delaware Canal – a locked, toll canal, privately owned and operated by the Chesapeake and Delaware Canal Company.

The monumental task of canal construction attracted workers to the area. Many settled around the western terminus of the canal, where a tan yard, a saw mill, and a wharf already were located. This small set-

The Engineer's Office at the Army Corps of Engineers complex (center), circa 1960. Canal Street, shown above-center, was removed during the canal-widening project of the early 1960s.

tlement was known as Bohemia Village, after Augustine Herman's estate. After completion of the canal in 1829, water traffic brought many visitors to the area, and the settlement began to grow. However, Randal's plans for a town at the mouth of Back Creek fell through, and he sold out and moved on. The area is still called Randalia.

The canal was cut through the north bank of Back Creek, creating an area that came to be called the Causeway. The town now had three distinct sections: the north side of Back Creek, the south side of Back Creek, and the Causeway between them. The High Bridge and the Long Bridge linked these areas. People made their homes on both sides of the creek and travelled easily throughout the town using these bridges. By 1839, the town had grown enough to warrant a post office, and had been given the name Chesapeake. In 1850, the town was incorporated as Chesapeake City.

The Chesapeake and Delaware Canal project was remarkably successful, and use of the canal exceeded all expectations. Steamships, carrying both freight and tourists, began using the canal in the 1850s. People travelled by steamship between Baltimore and Philadelphia on excursion lines which provided continuous service between the two ports. Chesapeake City was a major supply stop and port of call. New businesses opened to support the influx of people. The water-oriented community became a desirable place to live as well as to visit. For the next seventy years the town thrived, and its population grew to 2500.

The influx of new residents extended to the outlying areas of Bethel, St. Augustine, Court House Point, Randalia, and Town Point. Visitors often returned to buy farms and property for vacation homes. Locals opened stores, operated saw mills, farmed, and pursued hunting and fishing occupations. As these "suburbs" burgeoned, one-room schools were opened and churches were established.

Roads and transportation were still primitive in the late 1800s. Travelling to Chesapeake City from outlying areas, such as Town Point neck, took a whole day by horse and wagon, with plenty of planning ahead.

People familiar with modern-day Chesapeake City would hardly recognize it as the same town in 1900. Muddy, marshy banks and narrow waterways bore little resemblance to today's leveed banks and wide canal. Most of the town's streets were dirt and some were covered with oyster shells to minimize mud and ruts. The waterfront area was the hub of activity and was lined with warehouses and docks to accommodate barges and workboats transporting a variety of goods.

The Chesapeake and Delaware Canal Company did not fare as well as did the town. The company encountered unforeseen expenses for upkeep and repair on its privately-run toll canal. Profits gradually decreased. About 1875 the company began negotiations to transfer C & D Canal ownership to the U.S. government. The transfer came to pass in 1919 and government officials decided to transform the canal into a free-passage, sea-level waterway. A canal improvement project resulted, and it dramatically changed the appearance of the canal itself and of the town of

NEWS FLASH

"The population of Chesapeake City has increased 287 in the last ten years, making it the second largest town in the county. The 1910 census returns were 1016, and that of 1920, 1303."

– Cecil County News, 1920

Bohemia Avenue Waterfront, 2000

Chesapeake City. The town was about to lose the identity it had held for several generations.

After the canal opened as a sea-level waterway, the old bridges were removed and a new lift bridge connected the town's north and south sides. Most of the Causeway was removed; the remaining part housed only government canal offices. People still travelled easily from north side to south side over the lift bridge, but things were different. Larger vessels now used the canal, and canal traffic did not stop in Chesapeake City as frequently as it once did. The wharf areas of town therefore lost their commercial value. By the 1920s, automobile replaced horse and wagon, and people travelled longer distances. Larger stores in larger towns drew people away from Chesapeake City, and its businesses suffered.

In 1929 the stock market crashed, and despite the town's remote location, Chesapeake City felt the effects. Businesses struggled to remain solvent, and changed hands often. The outlying areas also suffered during the 1930s. People lost farms and saw their livelihoods shattered, but by the end of that decade the town began to revive.

In 1942 a German freighter rammed and destroyed the lift bridge at Chesapeake City – an event with profound consequences for the town. Ferry service was provided until a new high-span bridge opened in 1949, bypassing the town. No longer could residents easily walk or travel from one side of town to the other. In the 1950s and 1960s, the canal was expanded to accommodate larger ocean-going vessels which typically bypassed Chesapeake City. Businesses closed, one after another, until by 1960 little was left of the bustling, self-supporting town of yesteryear. Houses

and buildings were left to deteriorate. Some of the outlying areas, however, no longer depended upon Chesapeake City, and experienced enormous residential growth – a trend that continues today.

In the 1970s, renovations of a few old structures kindled interest in revitalizing the town. Over the next twenty years, restoration of the waterfront area drew tourists back to Chesapeake City, and the town once again began to flourish.

Today, the city dock is occupied not by commercial vessels but by sailboats, power-boats, and other small pleasure craft bringing visitors and shoppers to town. Businesses once again thrive, but by offering seafood and local memorabilia instead of wagon wheels and straw hats. Homes have been restored and the town of Chesapeake City has a new "old" look. Most of its 1500 permanent residents work and shop in larger towns.

The town and the canal enjoy a new relationship today. Once again, Chesapeake City thrives.

"One day in the 1970s, some entrepreneur may develop the town to its potential with the skillful addition of a few restaurants or cafes, shops and lodgings for tourists."

– Baltimore Sun, 1959

The Causeway

Some have said the most beautiful part of Chesapeake City was the willow-lined road on the Causeway.

The Causeway, once known as Whig Island, was a spit of land between Back Creek and the Chesapeake and Delaware Canal, connected by bridges to the north and south sides of Chesapeake City. The Causeway road enabled the residents to travel easily from one side of town to the other.

The Canal Company's waterwheel and associated buildings, the Masonic Hall, a doctor's office, the town's first fire house and a few homes were located on the Causeway.

Willow-lined Weir Street, on the Causeway, circa 1870.

When the canal was widened to a sea-level waterway, most of the Causeway's land was removed. Today, the Corps of Engineers Office and Canal Museum are all that remain there.

Photo courtesy of U.S. Army Corps of Engineers

ABOVE: An early-1900s view of the Causeway from Bohemia Avenue.

LEFT: Buildings housing the water-wheel and steam pumps, located on the Causeway, circa 1880. The raceway carried water from the waterwheel under the fence to the canal.

Photo courtesy of
Mr. & Mrs. John Sager

The Canal

Steamship in the Canal

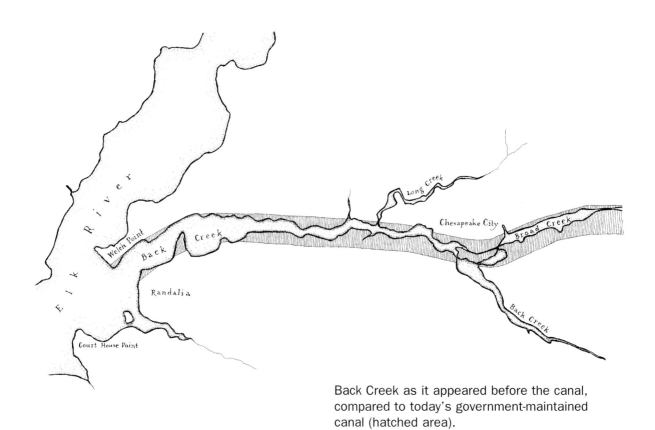

Back Creek as it appeared before the canal,
compared to today's government-maintained
canal (hatched area).

The digging begins . . .

The C & D Canal was dug and maintained by the Chesapeake and Delaware Canal Company. For ninety years (1829-1919) it was privately owned and operated as a locked, toll canal. In cutting through the northern Delmarva peninsula, the canal took in the creek beds of Broad Creek, near the peninsula's western border, and St. George's Creek, near its eastern border.

The canal was constructed before the era of mechanization by men wielding picks and shovels. Workers filled barrels with earth and pulled them up the banks of the canal using ropes and sometimes mules. If the grade was not too steep, horses pulling scoops (metal boxes with handles) were used.

Excavated mud from the marshy creeks was deposited along the canal's banks. The soft banks were difficult to stabilize, especially through the area of the "Deep Cut" between Bethel and St. George's, where the canal banks were quite steep. At the Deep Cut, the canal was dug through a ridge in the peninsula, where as much as 75 vertical feet of earth had to be removed.

As many as 1500 men were employed at the height of the construction. Many of the laborers were of Irish or African American descent. Most lived in shanties along the canal's banks, while others established residence in Bohemia Village, at the western terminus of the canal. The "village" consisted only of the canal lock house and a tavern.

The new canal was little more than a glorified ditch, but it served well its purpose of a safer, faster passage between the Chesapeake and Delaware Bays. When completed, the canal had a channel thirty-six feet wide and ten feet deep.

The canal traversed land which was above sea-level, and therefore required a system of locks. A lock operated as fol-

Chesapeake City

lows: a boat entered the empty lock through a swing gate; water was added to the lock to raise the boat to the canal's water level; the drop gate at the other end of the lock was raised, and the boat exited the lock. The process was reversed at the other end of the canal. There were four locks in the canal at its completion in 1829 – two at Chesapeake City, one at St. George's, and one at Delaware City. The locks were ninety-six feet long and twenty-two feet wide. They held eight feet of water over the sill (bottom of the drop gate), and were constructed of wood and granite. The granite for the locks was quarried in Port Deposit, in the northern part of Cecil County. The lock at Delaware City is still intact, although it is no longer in use and is not part of the present canal.

Schooners, barges, and other vessels were towed through the canal by mule teams, which walked along the north bank of the canal. A barge could be towed from Chesapeake City to Delaware City in four to six hours, depending upon the aptitude of the captain of the vessel being towed and upon the number of mules used. By 1870, steam tugs were used routinely to guide or tow. Mule teams were last used for towing

in 1902.

Maintaining the water level in the western end of the new canal was a constant problem. Although fed by ponds and streams, the canal was often too low in dry seasons to allow passage. A full lock of water was lost each time a boat passed through the lock in Chesapeake City. The canal was deeper east of St. George's, so the water level was not an issue in that area.

Mule Driver

. . . in 1959, Harry Borger, the only person left in Chesapeake City to have handled the mule teams on the canal, said:

"A team of mules usually was four, but we'd add another if the cap'n of the vessel paid extra, only three mules if the vessel was small. When we got tired of ridin' the mules, we'd get off and walk, and pick berries along the way."

– *Baltimore Sunpapers*

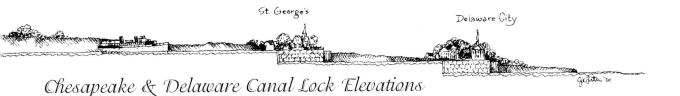

St. George's

Delaware City

After 1837, a steam pump installed at Chesapeake City pumped water from Back Creek into the canal when the water was low. In periods of heavy rainfall, excess water was drained through the waste gates, located east of the steam pump in Chesapeake City. The overflow drained into Back Creek.

The water in the canal was brackish (not as salty as the bay water); therefore, the canal froze and was un-usuable for part of each winter. When it froze hard, Chesapeake City folks packed a lunch, donned their skates, and skated to Delaware City – a twenty-four mile round trip.

The wooden lock gates were prone to damage from ice in winter and from the impact of boats entering the locks. The canal closed periodically to enable workers time to clean and repair the locks. A diving bell, built in 1839 in Philadelphia, was used as an air chamber for workmen making underwater repairs to the lock gates (see drawing on page 17). A man crawled underneath a large domed container which was open at the bottom. When lowered into the water, the container held enough air to allow the man time to make the

Ice Skating

Wintertime fun:

"She's harder than a brick bat, and no cracks! Let's go!" may have been heard from the youngsters in Chesapeake City when the ice was just right for skating.

Ideal ice, especially for a pick-up hockey game, was called black ice. Black ice formed when the temperatures plummeted, in absolutely windless conditions. The ice was so clear as to be nearly transparent, with not a hint of a ripple anywhere.

Boat coming out of Lock, Chesapeake City, Md.

Schooner navigating the Chesapeake City lock, circa 1900. The mules were used to pull vessels through the canal.

Chesapeake and Delaware Canal at Chesapeake City, circa 1860. The men are standing on the Causeway. The High Bridge and steam pump are in the background.

Photo courtesy of U.S. Army Corps of Engineers

necessary repairs. The diving bell is on display today in Delaware City, near the original canal lock.

Operation of the canal was a constant financial challenge for the Canal Company. Through the Deep Cut, earth slides were often a problem. The slides played havoc with the channel depth, sometimes decreasing it to six feet or less. The canal had to be closed until it could be cleared for passage. At these times money was spent for repairs, while none came in as tolls.

By the 1850s, with canal traffic increasing, further improvements were necessary. Schooners, passenger and freight barges, and lumber and coal scowls kept the locks busy. More water was routinely lost from the canal than could be replaced by the steam pump. In 1852, a water-lifting wheel was designed and put into service to maintain the canal's water level. Because the wheel was needed nearly twenty-four hours a day, in 1854 a second steam pump was added and the water-wheel was reinforced. The waterwheel and steam pumps operated for the remaining time the canal was locked (1854-1927).

Shipping companies were building larger cargo vessels, and increased clearance

NEWS FLASH

"A large rock went through the home of Charles Keithley during the blasting of the old locks."

– Cecil County News, 1925

Diving Bell

through the locks became necessary for these boats to use the canal route. The canal company replaced the old locks with a larger one, 220 feet long and twenty-four feet wide. The canal was re-routed 200 feet north of the old locks at Chesapeake City. A saving basin was dug on the north side of the lock to hold extra water for the canal.

By the 1860s, the regionally-significant canal took on national importance as well. In 1864, Union troops from Delaware, Pennsylvania, and New Jersey were moved to Washington, D.C. via the C & D Canal, arriving in time to defend the capital against a Confederate seige. Travelling by way of the canal

The Chesapeake and Delaware Canal at the Railroad Bridge, looking west. Note the mule tow path and telegraph lines on the north side of the canal. The telegraph lines were installed in 1860 to provide better communication between Chesapeake City and Delaware City.

Photo courtesy of Mr. & Mrs. John Sager

allowed the army to bypass Confederate land troops blocking road access to the capital. That single maneuver is given credit in many sources for preventing the fall of Washington, D.C.

Profits steadily decreased for the Canal Company during the second half of the nineteenth century. In 1875, the Atlantic Deeper Waterways Association, on behalf of the canal company, began negotiations for U.S. government purchase of the canal. In 1919, the government took control of the canal and made the decision to convert the canal to a sea-level, free-passage waterway.

The sea-level canal was ten years in the making. The project was accomplished without interrupting canal traffic, which averaged fifty vessels per day. This major overhaul of the canal began in 1921 with dry excavation just east of the old Canal Company office at Chesapeake City. Workers laid a railroad track in the dry excavation bed to help speed the earth-removal process (see photo on page 25).

Photo courtesy of National Archives.

Steam tug with a tow of barges hauling railroad ties, heading east on the Chesapeake and Delaware Canal near Summit Bridge, circa 1880.

View west from the High Bridge at Chesapeake City, circa 1880, showing the wooden fender used to help guide boats around the turn and past the bridge. The lock is located beyond the boat tied at the wharf.

Toll on commodities through the canal:

- ◆ *1¢ per bushel for grain*
- ◆ *$12 per boatload for fresh fish*
- ◆ *Loaded unchecked boats:*
  $6 per boat
- ◆ *Most other cargo:*
  less than 50¢ per whit
- ◆ *Empty vessels:*
  $4 per transit

Full vessels may repass toll-free within 30 days

NEWS FLASH

"Atlantic Deeper Water-ways Association: 'The acquisition of the canal is one of the first steps toward a plan for a series of waterways extending all the way from Charleston, SC, to Boston and including the Cape Cod Canal, near Boston, dug recently.'"

– *Cecil County News,*
August 1919

Dredges, used for wet excavation in most of the canal, were unable to navigate the lock at Chesapeake City. To address this problem two cofferdams, made of steel sheet piling, were constructed in the saving basin. These could be removed and replaced to allow the dredges to enter the canal, bypassing the lock. The working plant for the canal expansion, according to the Philadelphia District Corps of Engineers overseeing the project, consisted of "seven large hydraulic dredges, two scoop dredges, one steam shovel and two dragline banking machines."

Dredging was a big job in the Deep Cut, where the banks reached a height of seventy-five feet above sea level. This required lifts of eighty to ninety-five feet to deposit the dredge spoils in an area outside the channel cut.

The new sea-level canal took the same course as the old locked canal, with the exception of a new entrance south of Delaware City. The canal's channel was ninety feet wide and twelve feet deep. New

bridges were built at Delaware City, St. George's, Summit, and Chesapeake City, and old bridges were removed. The old bridge at Bethel was not replaced.

Annual freight tonnage increased by one hundred percent in the first six years after the new canal opened. The government soon recognized the need for a still deeper, wider channel. In 1933, when thousands of people were out of work and on relief after the stock market crash of 1929, the project was proposed. The canal-widening project was approved in 1935.

The Emergency Relief Appropriations Act, put into place by the U.S. government, stipulated that ninety percent of those hired for government jobs were to come from the relief rolls. As many as 2500 men worked on the C & D Canal project during the 1930s. Powerful pipeline dredges – *Baltimore*, *General*, *Orion*, and *Ventnor* – were brought from Baltimore to excavate thirty-five million cubic yards of earth from the channel. Bank-stabilization problems through the Deep Cut required a study of bank soils and a new plan of

NEWS FLASH

"The opening at the steam pump where the water is forced into the canal is filled with herring and a small boy spends his leisure hours with his dip net landing them. Sometimes the entire bank on either side of the water is covered with herring. The stream has to be cleared as they would get into the wheel and thus prevent it from running."

– *Cecil County News,*
May 1897

action. The new design called for flatter slopes and a drainage system to carry away surface water. From 1940 through 1948, six and one-half miles of the canal's banks were terraced using this new method. In addition to the existing canal channel, a new twenty-six mile approach channel was dredged. It extended from the mouth of Back Creek to Poole's Island, in the Chesapeake Bay. When dredging was completed in 1938, the C & D Canal had a channel 250 feet wide and twenty-seven feet deep at mean low water. What remained of Broad Creek, east of Chesapeake City, was filled with dredge spoils and made into levees. Large ocean-going vessels were now able to use the canal passage.

Despite the deeper, wider channel, freighters still had difficulty navigating the sharp curves in the canal, and often ran aground. Also, low clearance at the lift bridges left little margin for error. In 1939, the lift bridge at St. George's was struck and demolished by the freighter *Waukegan*. In 1942, the Chesapeake City bridge was similarly brought down by the freighter *Franz Klasen*. Ferry service was begun for highway traffic until new bridges could be erected. The need for yet another canal expansion project was apparent.

Studies by the U.S. Army Corps of Engineers, completed in 1954, made these

Photo courtesy of National Archives.

Dredge entering the saving basin through the cofferdam at Chesapeake City, circa 1922.

recommendations: a new high-span bridge at Summit; dangerous curves straightened at the railroad bridge and at Chesapeake City; a channel 450 feet wide and thirty-five feet deep at mean low water; a new high-level highway bridge at Reedy Point; bank stabilization (requiring grading, seeding, and drainage, with stone revetments); and lighting along both banks of the entire canal.

The government began to address these recommendations in 1958. Levees were established along the entire lengh of the canal from Randalia to Delaware City – thirteen and one-half miles. Dredge spoils filled Hog Creek, west of Chesapeake City, and Herring Creek, near Randalia. Cabin John Creek and Pierce Creek, farther down the Elk River, were also filled with dredge spoils.

Work was essentially completed by 1977. After this final widening, the canal completely replaced Back Creek from Chesapeake City west.

The Chesapeake and Delaware Canal of today bears little resemblance to the old locked canal. The wider, straighter canal has an engineered appearance, with riprapped shorelines and graded banks.

In this year of 2000, the Port Authority of Baltimore is encouraging enlargement of the channel once again. Debate is ongoing regarding the environmental impact of such a project on the canal and Chesapeake Bay.

NEWS FLASH

"The C & D Canal, beginning at Chesapeake City, at the upper part of the Bay and extending to Delaware City on the Delaware Bay has at last been taken over by the Government and is no longer a private enterprise, operated largely for the benefit of one line of steamers."

– *Cecil County News,*
August 13, 1919

DID YOU KNOW?

Willard B. McConnell is the only person known to have swum the Chesapeake & Delaware Canal from Delaware City to Chesapeake City when the locks were in place. He accomplished his feat in 1915.

TOP: Dredge working in the Deep Cut near Summit Bridge, circa 1920.

BOTTOM: Dredge at work in the Deep Cut, circa 1935. This was one of five dredges brought into the canal through the cofferdam.

Dry excavation near the resident engineer's office at Chesapeake City, circa 1921. The present-day canal occupies the area between Masonic Hall (left) and the A-frame of the bridge (right). The lock is to the right behind the steam-shovel.

Photo courtesy of National Archives.

Photo courtesy of National Archives.

C & D Canal, looking east from the Lift Bridge at Chesapeake City, in 1927. The lock, at lower left, was removed later that year.

The *U.S.S. Sandoval* navigates the Chesapeake City lock, circa 1899. The vessel was captured by the Spanish when Santiago, Cuba, fell during the Spanish-American War.

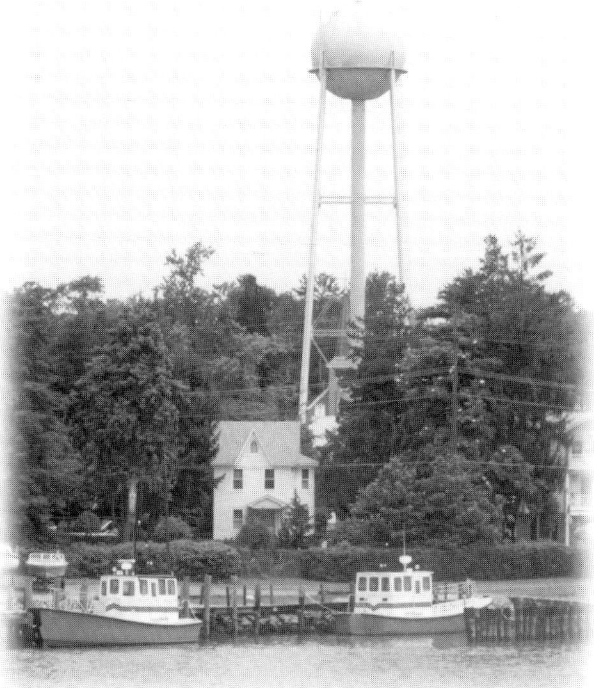

ABOVE: The boats of Pilot Transfer, Inc. docked near Schaefer's Canal House Restaurant, July 2000. These boats are used to exchange pilots on large ships.

NEWS FLASH

"Little Mary Carter, daughter of Mr. & Mrs. Bert Carter, Bohemia Ave., had a narrow escape from drowning while in bathing on Thursday afternoon. Since the dredging, there are very abrupt drops in Back Creek and Mary ventured beyond her depth and but for the timely assistance of Noble Benson, Jr., would have drowned, as she had gone down for a second time. Noble was on the bank in street clothes, but dashed in to the child's rescue."

– Cecil County News,
July 22, 1925

Today's sea-level canal provides a tidal range of 2.2 feet at the Elk River entrance and 5.2 feet at the Delaware City entrance. High- and low-water elevations are reached about two hours later at the Delaware River end than at the Elk River end. Due to these differences in elevation, the currents in the waterway vary in speed and direction, with a maximum current of 1.5 to 3 miles per hour.

TOTAL COST FOR THE 1927 SEA-LEVEL CANAL WAS:

$10,060,000.00

Photo courtesy of National Archives.

ABOVE: Waste gates, circa 1900. East of town, these gates helped control the water level of the locked canal.

BELOW: Building housing the waterwheel, circa 1890. The tall steel stack was used to improve the draft of the boiler.

STEAM PUMP, CHESAPEAKE CITY, MD.

Photo courtesy of Mr. & Mrs. John Sager

Steam Pump & Waterwheel

Water levels in the canal between St. George's and Chesapeake City were a continual problem because no tributaries supplied water to the canal in this stretch. Water was lost mainly through the lock at Chesapeake City, but also through breaches in the canal's banks. Therefore, a means to lift water from Back Creek into the canal had to be devised.

In 1837 a steam-operated pump was installed at Chesapeake City to raise the water from Back Creek. In 1852, after the larger lock was installed, the steam pump was unable to pump a sufficient amount of water to replace that being lost through the lock. The Canal Company made the decision to add a wooden scoop wheel, to be powered by the steam pump. Samuel Merrick and John Towne submitted a waterwheel design to the Canal Company. The waterwheel was built to the company's specifications by Merrick and Son. It operated exceptionally well, without overriding maintenance costs.

In 1854, Merrick and Son was hired to add another steam pump. The engine was a condensing steam-pump type with a Stevens valve gear, capable of producing 150 to 175 horsepower at 52 p.s.i. steam pressure. A second engine house was built, this one east of the wheel. The waterwheel, now sandwiched between the two steam engines, was itself reinforced and strengthened.

The waterwheel, made of wood and iron, was 39 feet in diameter and 10 feet wide, and had 12 lifting buckets. Water from Back Creek flowed into a deep trough under the wheel and its twelve buckets lifted the water to an upper race, or channel, through which it flowed into the canal about 960 feet east of the Chesapeake City lock. The water wheel lifted 227,000 cubic feet of water per hour, or 170 tons of water per minute.

The old wrought iron tubes on the steam pumps were replaced in 1865 by a pair of locomotive boilers, which gave 30 years of service. In 1895, Pusey and Jones, a shipbuilding

DID YOU KNOW?

In 1855, a man was killed while repairing one of the cylinders of the steam pump engine. As the piston was pulled from the cylinder, it was tied off. A man climbed into the cylinder to make repairs. The rope broke, dropping the piston and crushing him.

Resident engineer Clarence Brown stands beside the steam engine used to power the waterwheel, circa 1965.

Photo courtesy of U.S. Army Corps of Engineers

"Pusey and Jones" Return-Tube Boilers.

company from Wilmington, Delaware, installed two large round return-tube boilers, which could generate 500 horsepower.

The waterwheel and steam engines continued in use until 1927, when the locks were removed and the plant shut down. Even after seventy-five years of service, the engines remained in remarkably good condition. Workers today claim that "if the steam engine could be fired up, she'd still pump." In 1965, the pump house, including the water wheel, was declared a National Historic Landmark.

DID YOU KNOW?

In 1927, Henry Ford, of Ford Motor Company, offered the U.S. government $1,000,000 for the steam pump and water wheel, with the intention of moving them to Detroit, Michigan for display. The government declined the offer, and the pump and wheel are now housed in the Canal Museum in Chesapeake City.

Steam Tugs

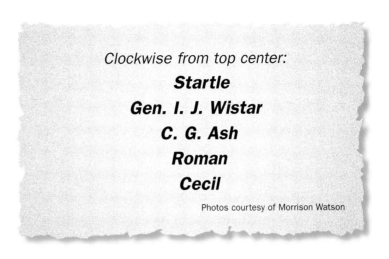

Clockwise from top center:
Startle
Gen. I. J. Wistar
C. G. Ash
Roman
Cecil

Photo courtesy of Rose Marie Hall Austin

Steamships

S teamships plied the waters of the East Coast in the late nineteenth and early twentieth centuries. The Baltimore and Philadelphia Steamship Co. inaugurated continuous waterway service between Baltimore and Philadelphia in 1844, with the C & D Canal as the major link. This ushered in a period of growth and prosperity for Chesapeake City.

The steamships were specifically designed with a narrow beam, shallow draft and no sidewheels. Sidewheels were replaced with Ericsson screw propellers. This new design enabled the boats to fit into the locks of the canal.

Well-remembered ships are the *Penn, Lord Baltimore, General Cadwalader* and *Richard Willing.* Other stops for

The *Lord Baltimore* excursion steamship locking through at Chesapeake City, circa 1908.

Travelling by steamboat was a pleasurable experience for many people, including this family aboard an Ericsson Line steamer.

Ericson Line 1906

these vessels were Tolchester, Betterton, Town Point, Lorewood Grove, and Delaware City. Steamships that completed their routes from Baltimore to Philadelphia in a day were called excursion boats; they carried primarily passengers, with freight below deck. If passengers congregated on one side of the boat, the boatmen below deck rolled barrels of water to the other side to keep the boat balanced.

The Ericsson Line, a Baltimore steamship company, was the largest revenue-provider for the

Portholes

"When steamboats entered the locks at night, us boys would all go down and stand on the lock alongside the boat so we could look in the portholes at the folks in their rooms. They couldn't see us 'cause it was dark."

- Chesapeake City resident

Chesapeake and Delaware Canal Company. The steamship line had a wharf at Chesapeake City, on the north side of the canal just west of Schaefer's store, where freight was loaded and unloaded. Passengers went ashore for refreshment and relaxation. In the summertime, the town's children offered cups of chipped ice flavored with strawberry syrup for five cents.

The steamship trip through the canal was leisurely and relaxing. In the early 1900s, lush greenery bordered the canal. A favorite stopping point was Lorewood Grove picnic area, between Bethel, Maryland and St. George's, Delaware.

Photo courtesy of Lisa Doricchi

Local residents watch as the steamship *Penn* navigates the Elk River on its way to Town Point, Chesapeake City, Lorewood Grove, Delaware City and points North, circa 1910.

Ticket book from Tolchester Beach Park, Kent County, Maryland. The amusement park was a popular stop for steamship travelers from the late 1800s until the 1940s.

White Crystal Beach, in lower Cecil County, circa 1950. This beach was one of many gathering places along the bay for dancing and summertime activities. Although it was not a stop for the steamships, many people travelled to White Crystal for its pristine sandy beach and its boardwalk.

Postcard courtesy of Mr. & Mrs. John Sager

DID YOU KNOW?

Tyrone Power, Irish comedian and great-grandfather of the celebrated 1940s movie actor of the same name, travelled on the steamboat *George Washington* from Frenchtown (near Elkton) to Baltimore in 1834.

Residents remember it as a cool, grassy area with large trees and a few picnic tables.

In winter, steamers occasionally became icebound in the canal. The passengers had to disembark and travel overland to the nearest town until the vessel could be freed.

Steamship travel and transport began to wane as more efficient means of overland transportation became available. Finally, the steamships could no longer compete and ended their passenger and freight service in the 1940s.

The steamer *Susquehanna of Baltimore* pulling away from Town Point Wharf, circa 1910.

Night Boat

"There was a night boat between Baltimore and Philadelphia, leaving Baltimore at 5 a.m. and arriving in Philadelphia about 9 p.m. Passengers received good meals, and it was comfortable. Folks would get on that boat in Chesapeake City, spend the next day shopping or visiting relatives in Philadelphia, then take the next boat back home. They'd get back early in the morning the next day. Could do that going to Philly. It was too long a trip to Baltimore. People only had a day or two they could be away from their work, they had to get back."

– Chesapeake City resident

The Town Point Wharf was a regular stop for steamships and schooners carrying freight and passengers. This 1910 postcard shows people awaiting the arrival of the next steamer.

NEWS FLASH

"The crew of the Ericsson line steamer attended the Presbyterian Church service. Captain Albert Willis accompanied the choir on the cornet."

– Cecil County News,
July 1926

"Several men from this place are working at Betterton, aiding in the building of the new Ericsson wharf. When the work is completed, they will build a new wharf for the company at Chesapeake City."

– Cecil County News,
July 1926

GOOD BATHING AT

BETTERTON

NO SEA NETTLES, DANCING, BOWLING, MOVING PICTURES AND ALL RESORT AMUSEMENTS. FISHING AND CRABBING.

– Cecil County News
August 1931

No. 5.   Steamer " Penn " on Delaware & Chesapeake Canal   John J. Kohler, Phila., Pa.

TOP: Steamship *Penn* carrying passengers through the Chesapeake and Delaware Canal, circa 1930.

BOTTOM: Steamship passing through Chesapeake City, circa 1941.

Bridges

High Bridge, Chesapeake City, 1900

Bridges

The new C & D Canal bisected the entire Delmarva Peninsula. The canal interrupted two north-south routes through Cecil County – the roads at Bethel and Chesapeake City. At the canal's completion in 1829, bridge construction began.

Bridges crossed the canal at Delaware City, St. George's, the railroad east of Summit, Summit, Bethel, and Chesapeake City. Two bridges at Chesapeake City, one across the canal and one across Back Creek, connected the two sides of the town.

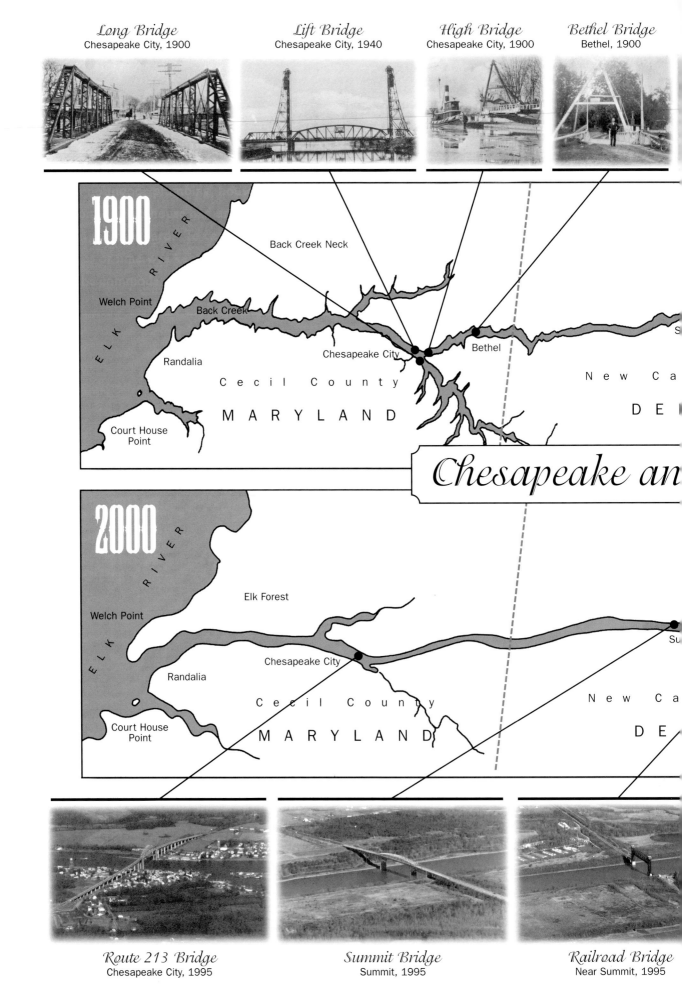

Long Bridge
Chesapeake City, 1900

Lift Bridge
Chesapeake City, 1940

High Bridge
Chesapeake City, 1900

Bethel Bridge
Bethel, 1900

1900

ELK RIVER

Back Creek Neck

Welch Point

Back Creek

Randalia

Chesapeake City

Bethel

Court House
Point

Cecil County

MARYLAND

New Ca

DE

S

Chesapeake an

2000

ELK RIVER

Elk Forest

Welch Point

Chesapeake City

Randalia

Court House
Point

Cecil County

MARYLAND

New Ca

DE

Su

Route 213 Bridge
Chesapeake City, 1995

Summit Bridge
Summit, 1995

Railroad Bridge
Near Summit, 1995

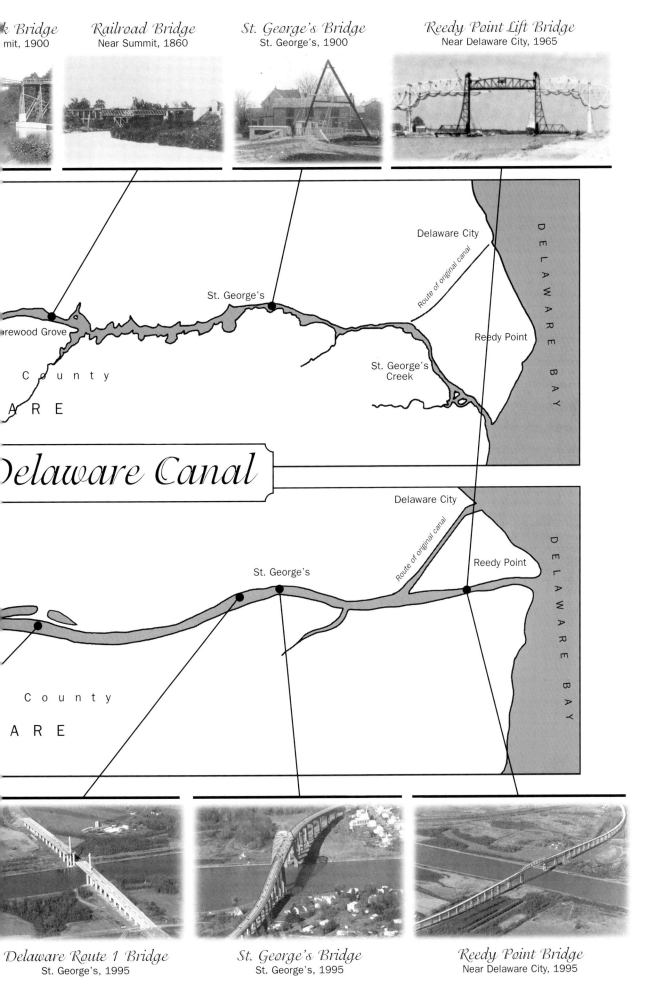

k Bridge
mit, 1900

Railroad Bridge
Near Summit, 1860

St. George's Bridge
St. George's, 1900

Reedy Point Lift Bridge
Near Delaware City, 1965

Delaware City

Route of original canal

St. George's

rewood Grove

Reedy Point

C o u n t y

St. George's
Creek

A R E

DELAWARE BAY

Delaware Canal

Delaware City

Route of original canal

St. George's

Reedy Point

C o u n t y

A R E

DELAWARE BAY

Delaware Route 1 Bridge
St. George's, 1995

St. George's Bridge
St. George's, 1995

Reedy Point Bridge
Near Delaware City, 1995

Long Bridge

The "Long Bridge," as it was called by locals, was the earliest bridge built at Chesapeake City. Its date of construction is unclear. Located at the foot of Bohemia Avenue, it bridged Back Creek and connected the south side of town with the Causeway. The wooden bridge had a span section which swiveled 180 degrees to let barges pass into and out of the Back Creek basin. A bridge tender opened the bridge by cranking a large horizontal wheel. The bridge had a wooden deck and an iron "draw" section. The iron side-railings of the draw span rose about eight feet above the deck. Many of the town's children used the bridge for a diving platform. "There was plenty of water in the creek when the tide was in, but you didn't want to dive off 'er at low water. It was great swimming there."

Long Bridge, Chesapeake City, Md.

Postcard courtesy of Mr. & Mrs. John Sager

High Bridge

At Chesapeake City, this bridge connected the north side of town with the Causeway road. It crossed the canal between the canal lock and the raceway of the waterwheel. This was a shear leg, or A-frame, bridge with a clearance of eight feet above the canal. The cabled frame lifted the wooden bridge deck by man-powered crank and swung it to the north bank to let vessels pass. "High Bridge" was the local name for this bridge. The High Bridge, combined with the Long Bridge, provided the link for the two sides of town.

Photo courtesy of U.S. Army Corps of Engineers

The High Bridge, circa 1900, looking east from the lock at Chesapeake City.

Photo courtesy of U.S. Army Corps of Engineers

View from High Bridge, looking west, circa 1900.

Pivot Bridge

Photos courtesy of Morrison Watson

ABOVE: Bridge tender Jim Watson at the Bethel Pivot Bridge, circa 1915.

RIGHT: Milton Watson stands beside the first vehicle to use the Bethel Ferry, circa 1927. His father, Jim Watson, ran the ferry after the Pivot Bridge was removed during the first canal improvement in the 1920s.

The A-frame bridge at Bethel was called "Pivot" by the area residents and was identical to the High Bridge at Chesapeake City. In the late nineteenth century, the road through Bethel was a major access route to Maryland's Eastern Shore.

In the 1920s, this bridge was dismantled after the canal-widening project. It was not replaced, and service across the canal at Bethel was scaled down repeatedly over the following years. A two-car ferry operated there until 1929, when it was replaced by a rowboat for foot traffic. This lasted just a few months before use dwindled and service was discontinued. As the years went by, the Bethel settlement faded. With the last canal-widening project in the 1960s, the church at Bethel was razed and the community all but disappeared. Today, only the cemetery and one house remain of the original community.

The Railroad Bridge

Delaware Railroad Company bridge across the C & D Canal just east of Summit, circa 1831.

Today's railroad bridge (right) across the canal was constructed in the 1960s after the canal was straightened. The railroad bridge from the 1920s, spanning the abandoned curve, is at left.

Summit Bridge

The first of five bridges at Summit, a wooden covered bridge 237 feet long, was built in 1828. A stone plaque dedicating the new C & D Canal was placed near the north pillar of the bridge along the canal bank.

The second bridge, built in 1868, was an iron Howe truss bridge which pivoted on cen-

ter. The stone plaque was removed from the canal bank and placed at the bottom of the bridge pier, facing east.

A third bridge replaced the truss bridge. It was built in the same location and utilized the same bridge pier, with the additon of ten feet in height (see picture below). Locals called it "Swing Bridge" and "Buck Bridge." This bridge was in place until 1927, when a lift bridge, similar to the one in Chesapeake City, was built. At that time, the stone plaque was removed to Chesapeake City and mounted on the front of the building which houses the old waterwheel. In 1963, a modern four-lane highway bridge was built at Summit, and is the one that crosses there today. Old-timers still refer to Summit Bridge as "Buck Bridge."

TOP: The wooden covered bridge at Summit is dismantled as the new bridge nears completion, circa 1868.

RIGHT: "Buck Bridge," the third bridge at Summit crossing, circa 1915. It was removed upon the widening of the canal at Deep Cut.

St. George's Bridge

Photo courtesy of National Archives

The first bridge across the canal at St. George's was a shear leg, A-frame design. When closed, it provided only three feet four inches of clearance above the water. The bridge was located at the end of the lock.

The second bridge at St. George's, circa 1926, was identical to the lift bridges at Chesapeake City and Reedy Point. It was replaced with a high-span bridge in 1941.

Delaware City Bridge

Photo courtesy of National Archives

The bridge crossing the canal at Delaware City, built circa 1830, was a shear leg, A-frame design identical to the others crossing the canal. It was at Fifth Street and provided a vehicle-crossing for local residents.

During the 1920s canal-widening project, the east entrance of the canal was relocated two miles south of Delaware City and a new lift bridge was constructed at Reedy Point. In 1960 it was replaced by a high-span bridge.

Lift Bridge

When the C & D Canal was widened in the early 1920s and the locks were removed, the low bridges at Chesapeake City were replaced by a new highway lift bridge. The new bridge connected George Street on the south side and Lock Street on the north side. This became the main route through town and many businesses relocated along it.

The bridge opened in 1927 and became the focal point of the town. When raised, the center lift span gave 140 feet of clearance above the canal at mean low water. The control house for the bridge tender was located on the lift span.

Children walked to school across the bridge. They rode the lift span (when they could sneak a ride), to watch ships pass beneath their feet. Residents recall the view from the bridge: "It was wonderfully cool in the summertime, and you could just see for miles and miles."

When the Lift Bridge at St. George's was destroyed in 1939, and the bridge tender killed, the control house on the Chesapeake City bridge was moved to the shore at the south end of the bridge. Most young folks no longer rode the lift.

In 1942, a German vessel rammed the south pier of the Chesapeake City bridge, bringing it down. Many people today recall the event vividly, and mourn it as the death knell of the town. In a manner of speaking, the town did change after the bridge was destroyed. No longer could both sides of town be accessed quickly and easily.

Immediately after the bridge fell, a passenger ferry, *Victory*, began service.

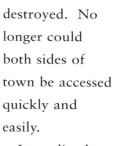

Photo courtesy of U.S. Army Corps of Engineers

TOP LEFT: Construction of the lift bridge piers, 1926.

BOTTOM LEFT: Dredging the channel under the lift bridge, circa 1927.

BELOW: The lift bridge as seen from South Chesapeake City, circa 1928.

It provided the only canal crossing at Chesapeake City until a vehicle ferry from New York State, *Gotham,* was brought to Chesapeake City many months later. With a thirty-five car capacity, *Gotham* provided the link across the canal from 1941 until 1949, when the current high-span arched bridge opened. Route 213 became the main route, and completely bypassed the town. As a result, traffic moved faster and more easily down the peninsula, and fewer visitors stopped in Chesapeake City. The town gradually declined over the next twenty-five years.

CHESAPEAKE CITY, MARYLAND

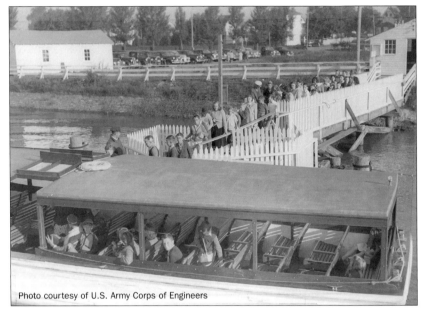

Photo courtesy of U.S. Army Corps of Engineers

LEFT: Chesapeake City residents boarding *Victory,* circa 1942. *Victory* was the first link between North and South Chesapeake City after the Lift Bridge fell.

BELOW: The ferry *Gotham* at Chesapeake City, circa 1942. When *Gotham* required service or repair, the ferry *Resolute* was used for passenger traffic.

Photo courtesy of Morrison Watson

LEFT: Wharf area on the south side of Chesapeake City adjacent to the ferry landing, circa 1947. Piers for the new high-span bridge are visible in the background.

BELOW LEFT: Cars in line to board *Gotham* at the ferry landing on the south side of town, circa 1947.

Photos courtesy of Lucy Titter

"The men that tended the bridges, they were the ones to talk to. 'Bout everybody that came by would chat for a while. Those men knew all the town's goings ons. They were better than a newspaper."

–Chesapeake City resident

DID YOU KNOW?

Howard's Pond, located near the canal at Bethel, was joined to the waterway around 1880 by a narrow inlet, over which the mule tow path crossed by a small bridge.

Home &
Family Life

Horse-drawn Sickle-bar Mower

Town Point Farm, 1925

Chesapeake City family life in the early 1900s was organized around subsistence. With money scarce for all but the wealthiest families, people worked hard just to make ends meet. There was no focus on acquiring luxuries or moving up in the world. People instead had to concentrate on food, shelter, and family. Self-sufficiency was a full-time job, as even the simplest chores were laborious, leaving little time for leisure activity. Still, most folks reflect that the hard work kept families closely knit. One resident put it simply: "We didn't *have* anything, but we had everything."

Money may have been tight, but there was plenty of fresh food right outside the door. Many families lived off the land, making use of the abundant resources in this rural area. Jobs were hard to come by, and people took whatever became available. Some men farmed; most supplemented their income and food supplies by hunting, fishing, and trapping. Farmers hired extra hands at planting, corn-thinning, and harvest times. Some people worked in the homes and yards of the wealthier families.

Bartering often replaced money in day-to-day business. People traded labor as well as goods. If someone needed a roof fixed, a shed repaired, or a wagon wheel replaced, the neighbors would help. A culture of honesty and cooperation sprung from this mutual dependence. "A man's word was as good as money in the bank," one resident reflects.

The earliest houses in town were built for canal workers in the mid-1800s. Small and economical, these houses were built several at a time and were known as "twelve foot houses" – one room wide and two to three rooms deep, with a second story and single-paned windows. Usually, the siding was clap-

NEWS FLASH

"Nine properties owned by the late Henry H. Brady, at Chesapeake City, were offered at the Court House door Tuesday morning by James F. Evans, Esq., but only four of them were sold, as follows: Lot on Third St. to William H. Johnson for $305. Lot and dwelling on Bank St. to John F. Carter, colored, for $40. Lot on Bank St. to Harry H. Griffin for $120. Lot and dwelling on Bank St. to Emma Carter, colored, for $170. Harold Steele was the auctioneer."

– *Cecil County News*,
1931

board and the interior walls finished with plaster and wallpaper. Some examples of these are still standing; many have been restored or remodeled.

With no indoor plumbing, houses had no bathrooms. Each house had an outhouse, or privy, in the backyard. To control odor, a container of lime was kept inside to sprinkle down the commode after each use.

Cleaning (removing the accumulated manure pile) was done every year or so, on the dark of the moon ("Wasn't as much to take out, the ground settled more"). As toilet tissue was an item yet-to-come, mail-order catalogs and corncobs were kept in the outhouses. Some farmers kept two bushels of corncobs in their outhouses: "One bushel of red cobs and one bushel of white cobs – you

A typical farming family at the turn of the century included several generations of family members. Seen here at a Town Point farm are women and children and the family hog, circa 1905.

used a red one, and then a white one to see if you needed another red one."

Electricity was not available in Chesapeake City until the mid-1920s, and some outlying areas did not receive electrical service until ten years later. Houses were commonly heated by free-standing, wood-burning chunk stoves, which were ususally located in a central room. The kitchen cook stove was also wood-fired. Larger houses had several fireplaces throughout, and some rooms were closed off and left unheated from late fall to early spring. Houses had little or no insulation. Sometimes newspapers were placed within the walls during construction, and these somewhat effectively kept the cold and wind at bay. Still, the heat was inefficient, especially in the upstairs sleeping areas. Floor registers allowed some heat to rise to the upstairs rooms, but not enough to make much of a difference in cold weather. One resident recalls, "Many a winter morning I'd wake up and see ice or snow on the inside sill of the window. Boy, did I hate to get out of bed those mornings! I'd run downstairs and

Critters

"My grandmother was a small, slender, tough little lady, hardened by outdoor work.

"One day, when I was just a youngster, we were walking toward the house, past the toolshed. Just under the toolshed door, my 'gams' noticed a rat's tail stickin' out.

" 'Shush, boy!' she told me and we stopped in our tracks. She crawled up on that rat real careful, grabbed him by the tail, swung him around and – bang! – up against the side of the shed. Killed him dead. She was somethin'."

– Chesapeake City resident

The chores of a spring day included cleaning and preparing the day's catch of perch. Circa 1915.

Sledding

"It was winter time, cold, with snow on the ground and ice on the river. My sister and I and a couple of other kids who lived in Port Herman were walking home from the one-room schoolhouse at the top of Pepper Hill. I was about 10. We decided we'd go down to the shore and play on the ice for awhile. We had our sleds, and we pulled them along with us out onto the ice. We had a big time playing for quite a while.

"When we got ready to leave, the tide had come in and the water was coming up onto the ice around the shoreline.

"There was no way you could get back to shore 'til the tide went out. I thought maybe I could get a running jump with my sled and shoot from the ice to the shore.

"Well, I fell right in that icy water. The kids laughed and laughed at me. I got so mad, I went on home and left them out there by themselves. It was nearly dark when Mr. Ulary heard the kids shouting 'Help! We can't get off the ice!'

"He came down the road and got 'em off the ice with an old row boat. Never did tell my mother what happened."

– Chesapeake City resident

NEWS FLASH

"'Bobbie' Walter is dead. 'Bobbie' was a faithful brown dog in the Walter family and was a familiar figure around town as he rode on the running board of the family car. 'Bobbie' will be greatly missed."

– Cecil County News, 1931

dress by the wood stove. Always slept good though, even though the room was cold. Had plenty of quilts and blankets to cover up with." By the 1940s oil-burning stoves replaced the wood stoves, eliminating a lot of the dirt and labor associated with burning wood.

Keeping the family fed occupied more daily time than any other chore. Homes had iceboxes for storing food items that were to be used quickly. Similar in shape and design to refrigerators, iceboxes held a block of ice in an inside compartment. The ice man made deliveries twice a week throughout town. For long-term food storage housewives pickled, salted, and canned fruits, meats, fish, and vegetables. Meats, milk and eggs were delivered door-to-door, or sold to the local grocery store by farmers for resale to the town residents. The town's local butcher delivered meat to homes from his store. "Mr. Hager delivered meat. My grandmother lived out of town, and she'd get all

the town news when he came 'round," remembers a local resident.

"In the old days, my gracious, everything took longer. Wasn't that things were harder to do, just more steps to do them," recalls a Chesapeake City native, now in his 80s. The daily chores necessary to run a household involved every member of the family, and kept the family members connected. Children learned to be self-reliant, but were ever under the watchful eyes and reprimanding hands of adult family members. "Seems like all we did was pump and haul water. The hand pump was out back and we all hated when it was our turn to get

School Shoes

One resident recalls . . .

"There was a family lived out of town, had three boys. Each one came to school for a week or so, and his brothers were absent. It went on quite a while until the principal finally asked their father why. He said the boys took turns going to school because they only had one pair of shoes. The principal went around town and rounded up enough money to get them all shoes. They all went to school after that."

Wagons

"Back in the '20s, there were more horses and wagons on the road than automobiles. I was really impressed with Mr. George T.'s wagons. He hauled fish, did threshing, and delivered stuff, and his wagons were the nicest ones. The wheels were about twice as wide as anybody else's wagon wheels. I really did like those wagons."

– Chesapeake City resident

A horse-drawn carriage pauses by the Elk River, circa 1906.

Photo courtesy of Lisa Doricchi

Rabbit Huntin'

"One old-timer in town used to like to go rabbit hunting. He had a couple of good rabbit dogs. He took another man in town, who had Parkinson's disease, huntin' with him. The man's arms and hands shook all the time. He always said, 'He can't hardly walk or hold still for a second, but when he raises that shotgun to aim at a rabbit, he's the calmest, best shot around.' "

– Chesapeake City resident

water on a cold winter day. Had to prime the pump (she nearly always froze up on a cold night) to break 'er loose. Took about three times as long to get her goin' in cold weather," reflects one resident.

Water was hauled indoors, heated if need be, and used for cooking, cleaning, laundry, and bathing. Typically, one day a week was set aside for laundry. A housewife spent many hours filling tubs with "wash water" and "rinse water," scrubbing the clothes on a scrubbing board, and hanging them to dry. Ironing was reserved for another day. The housewife had to heat cast-iron flat irons on the wood stove. Scorched shirts and burned hands were hazards of this method.

Bathing was a brief affair, not the leisurely shower or tub bath we enjoy today. Each bedroom had a porcelain wash bowl which held about a gallon of water. People hand-bathed in this fashion. A large tub in the kitchen was occasionally filled to provide a legitimate "tub bath."

"We'd walk through the woods to the marsh along Back Creek. We'd push a stick about 2 or 3 feet long down in the mud and tie a string to it. Then we'd tie a piece of bait, and a big bolt for a weight to the other end of the string. Caught many a crab that way."
– Chesapeake City resident

"I wanted to go to town on my bicycle, but she had two flat tires. Didn't have any money to buy new tubes for 'er, so I figured I had to do something. It was too far to walk. I got a funnel and spent quite a few hours filling the tires with sand. It worked. She rode rough, but she rode. Took all day, but I got to town."
–Rural resident

Because of their relative isolation from town, farm families were necessarily more self-sufficient. They were far enough out of town to be out of reach of goods and services on a daily basis. Farmers went to town by horse and wagon two or three times a month for supplies and to visit friends and relatives.

Few farmers could afford to own their own places. Most were tenant farmers, tilling the land for absentee owners. Many moved from farm to farm every couple of years "to try to get a little better farm – get a better yield and make a little more money. Once in a while a farmer did well enough to be able to buy his own farm," reflects a retired Chesapeake City-area farmer.

Farmers grew crops, milked cows, raised poultry and hogs, kept large kitchen gardens, and processed their own meat. Some had berry patches and grape arbors. Chickens supplied the farm family with eggs. In most cases, the farmers' wives tended the poultry, gathering and selling

Timber Rafts & Decoys

A raft of timber arrives in Chesapeake City, circa 1900. Left to right are Elmer Watson, Mallory Toy, Harry Vance, Jim Watson and Ed Reynolds.

Photo courtesy of Morrison Watson

The Susquehanna River was used by logging companys of New York and Pennsylvania to float large rafts of timber from the forests to the sawmills downstream. These rafts were broken up at the mouth of the Susquehanna River, where blemished logs were discarded and set adrift. Good wood was barged west down the bay, or east through the canal. Local residents took advantage of the discarded logs – especially white pine, which they found to be of ideal weight for making decoys. Local carvers on the Susquehanna, North East, and Elk Rivers in the 1800s and early 1900s were renowned for making working decoys for waterfowl hunters. Their decoys have since gained world-wide acclaim.

Mr. Jim Watson, of Chesapeake City, took the last raft of logs through the Chesapeake and Delaware Canal. His son, Milton Watson (1911-1985), was a well-known carver of working decoys and miniature gunning rigs.

eggs and feeding, killing, dressing and cooking the birds. Some wives also helped with the milking. Cows supplied the farm family with fresh milk and with cream to churn into butter. "That home-churned butter was sure good, but land sakes, it did tire out the arms. We didn't complain near so much if we was churnin' ice cream," says a local resident. Farms had root cellars for the winter storage of potatoes and other root vegetables. These were rooms approximately twelve feet square and twelve to fifteen feet deep, with dirt floors and roof eaves even with the ground.

In the 1860s, the county established a public school system. One-room schoolhouses dotted the countryside around Chesapeake City to provide for the children in the outlying areas of town. Several residents recall one- to three-mile walks to attend school. Comments one former student, "Farm chores and a long walk to school soon worked off the six or eight eggs and quart of milk a kid might have for breakfast."

Leisure time was rare and cherished, and usually spent in family gatherings and in church activities. Tent revivals were commonplace in the summertime, as were travelling shows. Folks enjoyed pastimes such as playing cards, checkers, or chess, throwing horse shoes, playing ball, dancing, and playing musical instruments.

Children were born at home, and the town's doctor delivered the babies if he could get there in time. Larger families had to rely on relatives and friends to raise some of their children. If parents became ill, the children were sent to live with relatives. In the close-knit community of Chesapeake City, children were known by the whole town. Everyone had a part in the protection of the town's children, as one resident recalls, "One day I went downtown to the movies.

"My father used to complain about the youngsters having it too easy, and no ambition. He said, 'A fat old rabbit dog isn't worth a darn. If you want him to hunt, you can't feed him the day before.'"

– Chesapeake City resident

"The room with the chunk stove was the place to be in the wintertime. All the other rooms would freeze water. My grandfather used to come in after workin' outside, take his clothes off down to his long underwear and curl up around the woodstove like an old dog."

– Chesapeake City resident

Oysters and the Bay Journey

"Pop was caretaker for Mr. Hemphill's property in Port Herman. He cut the grass and took care of the place; he also took care of the yacht. Mr. Hemphill had a really nice yacht for those days. She was maybe a 40- or 45-footer. One weekend, Mr. Hemphill told Pop he was bringing some people down to visit and that he wanted Pop to ready the boat for a trip down the bay to St. Michaels.

"Pop wasn't much on overnighters because the weather was unpredictable, or there might be engine trouble. He tied a bateau to the stern of the yacht, just in case. They had a nice trip down, spent the night in St. Michael's harbor and started back the next day.

"On the way up the bay, Mr. Hemphill noticed an oyster boat tonging oysters a ways off and told Pop to pull up alongside her so he could get some fresh oysters. Pop did, and Mr. Hemphill bought enough oysters to fill up the bateau.

"On the ride back, Mr. Hemphill started shucking some oysters for his guests, when he let out a loud cry. Well, don't you know, he gouged that oyster knife right in his hand. They tied a rag around his hand and got the bleeding stopped and continued on back to Port Herman.

"When Pop got the yacht back to the Hemphill's dock, Mr. Hemphill said, 'I want you to take that bateau full of oysters and dump 'em overboard.'

"Well, sure enough, Pop did. I guess Mr. Hemphill lost his craving for oysters that day."

– Chesapeake City resident

I wasn't supposed to leave the house, but a couple of friends said, 'Your Mom isn't even home, she'll never know.' Of course, she found out. Couldn't go anywhere for a week after that. Puzzled me how the devil she knew. When I was older, I found out the neighbor up the street told her. People were like that."

Older folks made their homes with their children, and the family often included other older family members as well. Parents did not discuss particulars with children about adult illnesses and hard times, but by being surrounded by older family members, children knew infirmities as a part of life. One resident recalls, "Uncle John would say something that didn't make any sense and us kids would just howl laughing at him. He died before I was grown, and later in life I came to know he had dementia. Folks died at home, and more often peacefully than not."

As the 1930s passed, the advent of electricity, modern transportation, and more industrialized farming methods shortened daily chores, decreased physical labor, and made available food and products that dramatically changed the focus of daily life. These changes gave people more leisure time. The old ways slipped away.

> *"We had unexpected Sunday company, with nothing, and I mean NOTHING, in the house to eat. My sister entertained the city folks in the sitting room while my mother went out back and killed, picked, and cleaned a couple of chickens. She brought them in, fixed them up, and we had a fine Sunday dinner. The guests never had an idea how their dinner came to the table."*
>
> – Chesapeake City resident

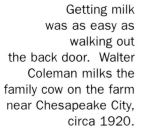

Getting milk was as easy as walking out the back door. Walter Coleman milks the family cow on the farm near Chesapeake City, circa 1920.

Catching herring on the Susquehanna, circa 1908.

Shutting Off The Marsh

On low tide, a line of stakes was driven into the mud flat at the entrance to the marsh. On high tide, when carp came into the marsh to feed, the fisherman fastened a net to the stakes, trapping the fish in the marsh. The carp were funneled into a pocket of net at one end of the stakes, in deeper water. The fish were dipped out of the net into live boxes. Mr. Toy, a Chesapeake City resident with a nearby pond, made a fortune selling the live carp to the Philadelphia-area Jewish population.

Another local fisherman recalls, "Pop and I tried the marsh way of fishing a couple of times. Man, was that a dirty, smelly job just to catch a few fish, and time-consuming too! We'd have to tow the live boxes from the marsh clear down to the Bohemia River, where we anchored them. If you went too fast, the water churnin' killed the fish. We had to putt-putt along about two miles an hour. It took us all day to get down the creek to the river."

Fishing

The creeks and rivers around the Chesapeake City area abounded with fish. Access to both the Elk River and the Bohemia River made the Town Point peninsula an ideal fishing area. Fishermen brought to market white perch, yellow neds, herring, shad, pike, catfish, eels, and carp.

In the early 1900s, most fishermen used pound nets. They laid out the nets in a rectangular fashion, about ten feet by fifteen feet, 200 to 400 yards off shore; a piece of net called a "hedging" extended from the pound net toward shore to guide fish into the net. Fishermen also used gill nets and haul seines. All of the net fishing required physical strength and endurance.

Crabs were abundant in the marshes around the area, and folks would catch a few – just enough to eat – with hand lines. There was no commercial market at that time for crabs.

NEWS FLASH

"The gunning season for yellowleg, black breasted and golden plover will open next Monday, August 16. The daily bag limit for yellowlegs is 15, and for black breasted plover 5. The season for squirrels, doves, rail and reed bird opens September 1. The daily bag limits are rail 50, reed 50, doves 25, squirrels 25."

– Cecil County News, August 11, 1926

YEAR 2000 Gunning Regulations

It is against the law to shoot yellowleg, plover, and reed birds (bobolink).

Bag limits:

RAIL......................10 per day
DOVE ....12 per day
SQUIRREL ....6 per day

Playing Ball

"Every Sunday, the Ukie boys and the coloured boys would play ball in old man Harriott's pasture. There'd always be a fight and a lot of name-calling. We'd see each other the next day in town and laugh about it. Next time Sunday rolled around, we'd have another ball game and another fight. We never stayed mad at each other, though."

– Chesapeake City resident

A Town Point farm, circa 1910.

Chesapeake City's
Ukranian Population

In 1910, a group of Ukranian people moved en masse from the central Pennsylvania coal-mining region to Chesapeake City to find a better way of life. Bishop Ortinsky, of the Philadelphia-area Catholic Diocese, saw the brutal working conditions endured by the Ukranian people working in the mines. On behalf of the diocese, he purchased 700 acres of land south of the Chesapeake and Delaware Canal for the Ukranian people to settle.

The C and D Canal project required many laborers, and in the 1920s many of the Ukranian men found work on the canal.

The Ukranian people are a unique part of Chesapeake City. The children of the first ones to settle here learned to speak English in school. Their parents, in turn, learned English from the children. They are Chesapeake City's only bilingual group.

The Ukranians' close-knit families, strict moral up-bringing, and pride in their surroundings have been admired by their neighbors for many years.

Surnames from the 1910 Ukranian Population of Chesapeake City

Ortynsky	Arkatin	Swyka	Blendy
Motowylak	Martiniuk	Onufreycuk	Luzetsky
Barahura	Wasylczuk	Pitel	Boyko
Hrabec	Tycki	Paslawsky	Kmet
Shestock	Loburak	Lysak	Andryshyn
Krochak	Lichowid	Zaborowsky	Basalyga
Stephaniuk	Waclawsky	Kutz	Kulyk
Hyrnick	Teresczuk	Ladnick	Maksyn
Chicosky	Losten	Korcheba	Starowsky

"Thrashin'" Wheat

Threshing was an annual labor-intensive farming chore, and always came at the hottest time of year. Even with a machine to assist with the threshing, it was grueling work.

A few men in the area owned threshing rigs. They hired out to thresh wheat for farmers who did not have their own machinery. The threshers made the rounds from farm to farm during the season, with a rig consisting of the thresher and an iron-wheeled tractor to run the threshing machine. Two men ran the rig. A good threshing operation depended upon skilled men running the rig and working in the fields. One resident who helped with a threshing operation recalls, "One old farmer used to go to Baltimore and bring up a pick-up truck load of black men to help. They had no idea where they were. He'd take 'em all home a couple of months later."

Before threshing could begin, the wheat had to be bound, shocked, capped, and pitched. The binder bunched the wheat into sheaves and bound them with twine. Two to three men came behind the binder and shocked the sheaves, stacking them together in a circular fashion. To cap the shocks, two sheaves were laid on top of a shock and turned back, petal-like. The caps kept the wheat dry if rain came before it could be threshed. Dry wheat provided the best quality grain. When the wheat was ready, wagons crossed the field while several men followed and pitched the shocks onto the wagon with long-handled pitchforks. A man atop the wagon stacked the shocks neatly. The wagons were loaded high, and pitching toward the finishing of a wagonload was back-breaking work. The wagons then carried the wheat to the threshing machine.

The threshing machine was placed in the field wherever the farmers wanted a straw rick. A couple of men pitched the wheat into the feeder and the machine separated the wheat from the chaff. The grain came out a chute near the bottom where two bags were attached. One man secured and refitted bags as necessary. The chaff was blown out a chute near the top of the machine and was directed by means of a rotating chute cover; a straw rick resulted.

A good threshing operation could thresh 2500 to 3000 bushels of wheat a day. It was a dusty, throat-parching job.

Wood

"Seasoned" wood was preferred for heat. Men who supplied wood for the townspeople felled trees and split the wood into stove-size pieces a few months before it was to be burned. That practice allowed green wood to thoroughly dry. Many people recall, "Burning green wood gummed up the chimney something fierce and was easy to catch fire. That's something everyone was careful of. If you had a chimney fire, chances are your house burned down." One area resident whose family cut wood recalls, "We cut, split and loaded wood on the wagon, then hauled it into town. We'd go down the alleys between the houses, and throw a load of wood in each back yard. We sold the wood for $3.00 a wagonload. I was sixteen years old before I realized my name was not 'Git Wood.' It was a back-breaking, tiresome job."

Steve Bordley, raised by the Titter family, at Bohemia House, circa 1915.

NEWS FLASH

"An attempt was made to rob the store of Joseph Schaefer & Sons, early Monday morning. Archie Foster noticed a light on in the store and called John Schaefer, who took a shotgun and started to investigate. Seeing that they were detected, the two men attempted a hurried get-away, when John fired and hit one of the men, Jack Gregson, of Lewisville, Pa, in the leg. His accomplice was able to reach his car and drove off, but not until his license number had been secured. The sheriff was called and pursued the car until it overturned and the driver escaped through the woods."

— Cecil County News,
March 1931

Hunting

Chesapeake City's outlying areas were abundant with game. Men hunted small game such as squirrels, rabbits, groundhogs, foxes, and racoons. There was a healthy market for both the meats and skins of these animals. Muskrats and terrapins, both marsh animals, also were lucrative catches in the marshy areas around the town. Muskrats, for example, were stocked in the town's grocery store and the meats sold for 25 cents apiece.

As soon as they were old enough to understand and strong enough to help, sons of hunters and fishermen learned hunting and fishing skills. Boys were able to make a little pocket money for themselves in this way: "We'd catch a few muskrats to sell, maybe get enough money to go and see a movie; the movie cost 15 cents," recalls one area resident. Deer were not common

Sinkbox Rig

in the rural areas around Chesapeake City in the early twentieth century. Venison was rarely eaten. One resident recalls, "Elk Neck had a lot of deer, but you just didn't see them on the east side of the river." Today, with huge cultivated fields of corn and soy beans, deer are abundant. A hunter today, utilizing all legal hunting methods, may take as many as twelve deer per year. Ducks were the main quarry of waterfowl hunters, although some sought other birds such as geese and swan. Duck hunting was a gainful way of putting money in the pocket as well as a delicacy on the table, and gunning for the market did not become illegal until 1918.

The mouth of the Susquehanna River, know as the "Susquehanna Flats," was the superior duck-hunting region of the Atlantic Flyway. The "Flats" is a broad, shallow area which was rich with wild celery (an aquatic grass) early in the twentieth century. That particular grass, which no longer grows on the "Flats," was a favorite food of the most delectable duck, the canvasback. Hunters were skilled at "reading the water" to determine if a given day would be a profitable hunting day. A former hunter recalls, "The old man could tell, even if it was foggy, if the ducks would likely decoy; don't know how he knew it, but he always predicted it right. When the ducks were migrating, the sky literally clouded over with thousands of them."

The waterfowl hunters used several methods to hunt ducks: blinds, bushwack rigs, and sinkboxes. For each method of hunting, decoys were placed on the water in the ducks' feeding area. A set of decoys was locally referred to as "a stool of decoys."

Over the years, the Susquehanna River area became famous for waterfowl hunting and for expertly hand-carved working decoys made by local residents. Some well-known carvers of the late nineteenth and early twentieth centuries were Ben Dye, John "Daddy" Holly, William Heverin, Paul Gibson, Scott Jackson, Sam Barnes, and Henry Lockard.

DECOY STOOLS

A "stool" of decoys refers to a set of decoys spread about in the water to lure the ducks to the hunter. The number of decoys required depended upon the hunting method :

BUSHWACK STOOL........100 - 125 decoys

BLIND STOOL....................50 - 100 decoys

SINKBOX STOOL ....200 - 300 decoys

Hogs

"In November, farmers killed hogs for the winter's meat supply. Neighbors came to help. Men would chase down the hogs and slit their throats, then let them stagger around until they bled to death. After that, the hogs were scalded and scraped to get the hair off the hide. Then they were butchered and made into scrapple, sausage, hams and lard. Us boys would wait around to get the hog bladders. We'd blow 'em up with a turkey quill, and have a great time kicking them around the yard. They made great soccer balls."

– Chesapeake City resident

Holes

"Always dug postholes on the light of the moon. Plenty of dirt left to fill around the post. On dark of the moon, you'd run out of dirt before the post was set tight in the hole."

– Local resident

ABOVE: Around the turn of the century, Port Herman was little more than a few seasonal homes and dirt roads. RIGHT: Elk River House.

Postcards courtesy of Lucy Titter

Port Herman Beach visitors used tents for overnight stays. Circa 1926.

Photo courtesy of Mary Anna Taylor

Port Herman

The outlying area of Town Point, including the settlement of Port Herman, became a vacation destination for visitors from Delaware, Pennsylvania and New Jersey.

"Elk River House," located at the end of Front Street, was a hotel for summer visitors run by William Fears in the early 1900s. It is now a private residence, and the present owner has occupied the property since the 1950s.

Port Herman Beach was established and opened for business on July 4, 1924. Amenities included a concession stand and tent sites for overnight visitors. Cabins were added later and rented by the season. The beach was a highlight for the area in the summertime until the 1960s, when it was closed and the property was sold. Around 1915 Port Herman had a small store on Cherry Street, and the area post office was just a quarter of a mile up the main road.

PORT HERMAN BEACH, CECIL CO., MARYLAND

TOP, CENTER and BOTTOM: Port Herman Beach, circa 1930.

Photos courtesy of Mary Anna Taylor

Chicken House

Sager's chicken house, as it stands today in South Chesapeake City.

John Sager's chicken house was full of old family stuff – stuff which had been kept, treasured, resurrected from dilapidation, and generously given out over the years to family and friends. The contents represented a history of several generations of one Chesapeake City family, and were stored there long after the chickens were gone. The weather-worn building still stands a short distance from the Sager's house, down a grape arbor-lined walk.

During the U.S. Army Corps of Engineers 1920s project to widen the C & D Canal, the lightkeeper's house near Randal Light was slated for demolition. This house was built of broadwidth hem-lock sawn from local timber. John's father, Jay Sager, bought the house at auction for $51.51. John and his father took

Sagers' early chicken house, built in 1911.

the house apart, piece by piece, and hauled it several miles through the woods and countryside to the Sager property on Basil Avenue. The men built their chicken house using the hemlock boards salvaged from the lightkeeper's house.

The Sagers raised chickens and sold both chickens and eggs for a number of years. Even before they were in the commercial chicken business, they had a few chickens, and according to John, "We traded eggs for groceries."

Today, the Sagers still have a couple of chickens running around the yard, but they are pets rather than food for the table.

Lightkeeper

Before the widening of Back Creek, vessels found it difficult to navigate treacherous Sandy Point without the aid of "Randal Light," a kerosene-fueled navigation light that sat atop a group of pilings near the canal channel. The lightkeeper kept the light fueled through the night. Each evening a five-gallon container of kerosene was carried down a long wooden pier from the lightkeeper's house to the light. The kerosene was carefully transferred to the light's well using a small brass pitcher and strainer. Randal Light was removed in the 1930s.

Randal Light was at the end of a pier marking Sandy Point, a narrow shoal across from Welch Point. This area of Back Creek is now part of the C & D Canal and Sandy Point no longer exists. Circa 1910.

Doctors

In the late 1800s, Chesapeake City had two practicing doctors: Dr. J.V. Wallace (circa 1877) and Dr. Wm. C. Karsner (who practiced into the 1910s).

Earliest twentieth-century physicians included Drs. Wilsey, Conrey, C. C. Laws and Smithers. Dr. Wilsey practiced at the location previously occupied by Dr. Karsner. Dr. Conrey's home and office were in a large porched dwelling on Bohemia Avenue and Third Street, across from the Methodist church. Dr. Laws started his practice in a house on the Causeway, later building a large stone home on Third Street. Dr. Smithers was a dentist whose office was on the second floor of J.M. Reed's Store, and later moved to his home. His home was in the second block of Bohemia Avenue. Dr. Smithers' house on Bohemia Avenue remained in his family for over eighty years.

Dr. VanNorden came to Chesapeake City to practice medicine in the 1920s after Dr. Wilsey died. He was a homeopathic doctor whose office was on Third Street

Dr. Davis began his practice in Chesapeake City in 1931, at the corner of Bohemia Avenue and Fourth Street. Both he and Dr. VanNorden made many house calls during their careers. After a few years, Dr. Davis moved his family and office to the corner of George and Third Streets. In later years, he made his home with

*Circa 1915 location of
Dr. Thomas Conrey*

Circa 1925 location of Dr. C. C. Laws

*Circa 1931 location of
Dr. Henry V. Davis*

1938-1978 location of Dr. Davis

his wife and children at Randalia. He served as Chesapeake City's doctor from 1931 until 1978.

Today, Chesapeake City has no resident doctor. The closest doctors are in Cecilton – ten miles south – and in Elkton – seven miles north.

Circa 1935 location of Dr. VanNorden

Circa 1890 location of Dr. Karsner Circa 1920 location of Dr. Wilsey

NEWS FLASH

"Dr. Henry Vincent Davis, who for the past two years has been resident physician at the James Walker Memorial Hospital, Wilmington, North Carolina, has located in Chesapeake City, with his office in the home of Mrs. Hugh Wright Caldwell, Bohemia Avenue and Fourth Street."

– *Cecil County News,* 1931

Home Remedies

Croup – *1/2 tablespoon of sugar with warm melted lard poured over. Instant cure!*

Earache – *Wrap hot tea leaves in a small piece of cloth and place in the ear.*
—or—
Blow a couple of puffs of cigar smoke into the affected ear. Instant cure!

Infected Finger (or other area) – *Bread & milk poultice (bread soaked in milk) wrapped in cloth. Apply to infection.*

Chest Cold – *Mustard Plaster. Make paste of dry mustard and flour and place between two pieces of cloth. Heat on the stove. Apply to chest for about ten minutes.*

Head Lice – *Wash head with kerosene. Wrap in towels for a couple of hours, then wash with vinegar and follow with soap and water.*

Warts – *"Pow-Wow" the wart by gently rubbing it with a penny at sundown and saying a few "magic words." Wart will disappear in several days. (People who can do this are very rare).*
—or—
Steal a piece of fat and rub it on the wart.

Drawing Salve – *Mix together 1 lb. of turpentine, 1/2 lb. of bees wax, 1 oz. of camphor (gum) and 1 pt. of cottonseed oil. Store at room temperature in jars with tight lids. Good drawing salve for splinters and such.*

NEWS FLASH

"Mrs. Arthur Biggs was bitten in the face by a horse a few days ago. An ugly gash was made over her right eye."

– Cecil County News, July 8, 1925

Cold – *Burn an old rag; mix the ashes with goose grease and put it on your chest and back. Also could use mutton tallow.*

Cough – *Make tea out of the leaves of catnip and mix with sugar.*
            –or–
Mix a spoonful of sugar and a drop of coal oil.

Pneumonia – *Put on the chest manure fresh from the cow.*

Headache – *Pull plantain leaves from bogs and make a wrap with vinegar, sugar and salt. Apply to head.*

Arthritis – *Keep a potato in your pocket until it turns black.*
            –or–
Drink a teaspoon of vinegar in the morning and a teaspoon at night.
            –or–
Wear a copper bracelet.

Fever – *Put fresh onion on the feet and the stomach.*

NEWS FLASH

"Leroy Watson, son of Elmer Watson of Chesapeake City had his left arm amputated at Union Hosital on Monday. The lad while playing in a stable several days ago fell and sustained a compound fracture of his arm. Blood poisoning developed and physicians deemed it necessary to amputate the arm to save his life."

– *Cecil County News,*
April, 1926

Shops & Shopkeepers

Businesses

Bohemia Avenue, circa 1900, when the streets of town were dirt and hitching posts were common.

While the shops in Chesapeake City today cater mostly to tourists, the vibrant business community in the late 1800s and early 1900s served mostly residents. People had to go no farther than town for everything they needed for home or business. Ice, dry goods, clothing, lumber, hardware, coal, wallpaper, lime, grain and carpet are just some of the items that were readily available. An 1877 advertisement lists a sample of goods supplied by an area store: *"Andrew Beasten, Jr. - Dealer in dry goods, hats, caps, boots, shoes, groceries, and everything usually kept in a first class country store. Cayot's Corner."* Freshly grown and raised products were provided locally by those who harvested them. Other goods and supplies arrived in Chesapeake City by water on barges or were brought overland by horse and wagon.

Businesses say a lot about the character of a town. A look back at those businesses present in the late 1800s and the early 1900s gives us a glimpse into the life of the town in that period.

Joseph Schaefer and Sons, Ship Chandlery and Grocery (circa 1910)

Joseph Schaefer worked for the Wooley and Bennett Lumber Mill until 1908, when he opened a store and warehouse on the wharf, at the entrance to the Chesapeake City canal lock. Schaefer's store and warehouse provided goods and services for boats and their passengers. Mr. Schaefer's children, John and Katherine, opened a restaurant there in the 1930s, which became noted on the Eastern Shore for its deviled crab and crab cakes. They also ran a store at the wharf.

The restaurant has undergone two expansions. An upstairs dining room was added in the 1940s, and the present waterfront restaurant was built in the 1980s. Schaefer retired in the 1980s and sold the property, but the restaurant still bears his name.

Jos. Schaefer and Sons, Ship Chandlery and Grocery, circa 1910. The C & D Canal lock gate is in the background. One private residence can be seen on the Causeway, right of the lock gate.

ABOVE:
Schaefer's
Market and
Restaurant, circa
1955.

LEFT: Schaefer's
Canal House
Restaurant in
2000.

"Punch" Harriott (left), "Sarah" the horse and her colt, and William T. Harriott in front of the Harriott Hotel, circa 1900.

Bayard Hotel (circa 1850)

Reputedly the town's oldest building, the hotel provided rooms and meals for people employed by the Canal Company. It was called Chick's Tavern. Sarah Beasten operated the business from 1845 until 1858, when Richard Bayard bought it. Under his ownership it became a popular hotel for tourists. William T. Harriott bought the property in 1899 and renamed it Harriott Hotel. Mr. Harriott kept a stable at his hotel for horses and mules, which he rented to customers. He owned a pasture on the west end of town, at the end of Third Street, where the animals grazed. When some were needed, Mr. Harriott opened the pasture gate and the horses galloped themselves downtown to the stable. Folks recall that they made quite a racket running through town on the oyster-shelled streets.

Mr. Harriott operated the hotel until 1930, when dwindling business and the Great Depression overwhelmed him, and he

Today, the Bayard House Restaurant sits on the waterfront at the end of Bohemia Avenue in South Chesapeake City. It offers a view of the C & D Canal.

shot himself in one of the hotel rooms. His son, "Punch," took over the operation after that. It was locally known as the "Hole In The Wall."

Albert Battersby owned the property from about 1960 until 1982, when Mrs. Richard C. duPont bought it. She oversaw extensive restoration and remodeling of the building. Renamed the Bayard House Restaurant, today it is well known for its Eastern Shore cuisine.

A Trip to Town

"Mother and I would hitch the horse to the wagon and head to town about once a week to stock up on things we needed around the farm and maybe do a little shopping.

"We'd leave early in the morning, and go to Mr. Harriott's. He would unhitch the horse and feed and stable her while we walked around town. Mother and I also ate lunch at Harriott's. It cost us 25¢ a piece and 25¢ for the horse, so Mr. Harriott's bill was 75¢.

"Then we would head back to the farm late in the afternoon. It took all day."

-Walter Coleman

Canal and Back Creek Towing Company
(circa 1895)

Canal and Back Creek Towing Company, located in the basin area of Back Creek, operated steam tugs to pull vessels through the locked C & D Canal. The towing company worked in the canal during a period when mule towing was winding down. In 1914, Southern Transportation Co. began using their own tow vessels. As that company provided ninety percent of the canal's tow traffic, Canal and Back Creek boats were no longer needed, and the company shut down in 1914.

Conrey's Store
(circa 1920)

Mr. Frank Conrey operated a general dry goods in a handsome brick building built around 1900 by the Conrey family.

Mr. Conrey also owned quite a few properties throughout the town, as well as a large farm in Town Point neck. The building today is known as Franklin Hall, and is owned by the town.

Deibert Brothers
(circa 1900)

Located on Long Creek, the company built barges for use in the locked canal. The business was sold and became Southern Transportation in 1913. Deibert Brothers also had a location in Elkton, Maryland where many barges were built for use on the canal.

Formerly Conrey's Store

Queck's Bakeshop
(circa 1910)

On the corner of Bohemia Avenue and Second Street, this shop sold baked goods and homemade chocolate confections. Reportedly, local resident Mrs. Rees bought one pound of chocolate each day for her own consumption. By the 1930s, this site became Bramble's Restaurant. Today, it still houses a restaurant business.

Tomato Cannery
(circa 1915)

The cannery, which operated in the late 1800s, had been shut down for several years. In 1897 it reopened to the cheers of the townspeople, as it provided much-needed employment.

Lime Kilns
(pre-1920)

Two kilns located near town processed oyster shells to make lime. Lime was used in the production of whitewash, a material commonly applied to clapboard buildings and out-buildings to refurbish them. At the time, paint was a most expensive product.

Photo courtesy of
Morrison Watson

Queck's Bake Shop, circa 1910. This structure still stands today in South Chesapeake City, and retains much of its original appearance (photo inset).

Rees' Wharf and Hardware (circa 1915)

The Rees home on Bohemia Avenue, built by Mr. Brady in the late 1800s, was one of the more ornately designed homes in town. In the early 1900s, the Rees family owned a wharf and dock business just behind the home, where many barges loaded and unloaded their cargo. The family also owned the hardware store next door. Mrs. Rees had a lingerie business in her home for many years.

ABOVE: Dwelling formerly the Rees home on Bohemia Avenue.

RIGHT: Building formerly Rees' Hardware Store. In 1932, it was the American Store.

Location of Mr. Rees' wharf office. It was barely large enough to accomodate Mr. Rees and his desk.

J. M. Reed's Store
(circa 1915)

John M. Reed's store was on the corner of Bohemia Avenue and First Street, and operated as a dry goods establishment. Folks recall purchasing "nice wallpaper from Mr. Reed." The building, vacant for many years, now houses a business once again.

Formerly J. M. Reed's

Hager's Butcher Shop
(circa 1920)

Henry Hager ran a store and butcher shop on the corner of Bohemia Avenue and First Street. Mr. Hager peddled his meat products around town and in the outlying areas. He

NEWS FLASH

"Albert Beiswanger has purchased a Fridgidaire cabinet for his restaurant as his ice cream is shipped from Philadelphia in thermos tubs. The ice problem has been solved for him."

– *Cecil County News,*
1926

drove his meat wagon to farms in Town Point about once a week. One former farm resident recalls Mr. Hager pressing the scale with his thumb when he weighed meat: "He made a fortune with his thumb." The Hagers lived in the house adjacent to the shop. The shop later became a pool room, and in the 1940s became Mewhiter's Drug Store.

Formerly Hager's house; shop occupied lot in foreground.

Chesapeake City Bank (circa 1902)

The bank was the only bank to serve this town for nearly 100 years. The bank building, which is now the Town Hall, is an imposing granite structure at the corner of Bohemia Avenue and Second Street. The Methodist Church and the Canal Museum are the only other granite buildings in town. Some things do not change with time, as seen by this bank advertisement in the *Cecil News* of 1918:

"deposit 2 cents the first week, 4 cents the second week, and increase the amount 2 cents each week thereafter for fifty weeks. The Christmas Club grand total realized will be $25.50"

Bouchelle's Mercantile
(circa 1900)

Henri Bouchelle operated a general store at the corner of Bohemia Avenue and Third Street. The store carried groceries, some dry goods, and general merchandise.

Photo courtesy of U.S. Army Corps of Engineers

Henri Bouchelle's General Merchandise

Ice Houses
(pre-1920)

Located on the banks of the canal and Back Creek, the houses were filled in the winter with ice cut from surrounding ponds and streams. The ice lasted as long as several months. One resident recalls from his boyhood that ice could remain frozen for over a year in these houses.

Ground beneath the ice houses was dug out about ten to twelve feet deep. As ice was put into the house, it was covered with straw, insulating it for long term storage.

Kibler's Ice House at the end of Bohemia Avenue was tended by George O'hrel.

Photo courtesy of Morrison Watson

Harry Kibler's Ice House, circa 1925

DRUG STORE OF S. S. SAWTELLE.   CHESAPEAKE CITY, MD.

Sawtelle's Drug Store (circa 1920)

Formerly Alexander's, Sawtelle's supplied the medicinal products for the town. The Sawtelle family lived in the apartment above the store. This site later became successively the A&P Store, Tatman's Legrand Grocery, and the Chesapeake City Post Office and Karbonik's Barber Shop. It remains a business location today, with its exterior largely unchanged.

Sawtelle's Drug Store, circa 1917 (above), and as it appears today (below). The building is located at Bohemia Avenue and Second Street.

CARPENTER'S STORE – Biddle Street.

MRS. PRYOR'S ROOMING HOUSE – At Hemphill and Canal Streets.

TOWARD LORRAINE'S GARAGE AND OIL BUSINESS – Canal Street.

TOWNSEND WALTER'S GARAGE – Hemphill Street.

MALLORY TOY'S APARTMENT HOUSES – Canal Street.

LINDSAY'S LUMBER YARD

CONREY'S, TINSMITH – On the northwest corner of Bohemia Avenue and First Street. Mr. Hemphill was a tin-knocker for Mr. Conrey. This building housed the town Post Office about 1930 (Kitty Schaefer, postmistress).

Formerly Beiswanger's

BEISWANGER'S SHOP – At the end of Bohemia Avenue, near Back Creek; in later years, the Beiswangers moved their business to George Street. Mr. Beiswanger delivered ice cream by bicycle to both the north and south sides of town.

CONREY'S COAL AND WOOD – On the waterfront at the end of Bohemia Avenue, on land later removed when the canal was widened in the 1920s.

HOUCK'S MILLINERY

MILTON TITTER'S GARAGE – In the second block of Bohemia Avenue, just north of Bungard's Store.

SAVIN'S CARRIAGE SHOP

HOWARD'S DANCE HALL

CHESAPEAKE CITY TEXTILE MILL

HUDSONS' BARBER SHOP – Run by brothers John and Willie, the shop was at the end of Bohemia Avenue. It was later moved to Second Street between Bohemia Avenue and George Street.

McKINNEY'S JITNEY SERVICE – Provided once-daily runs from Chesapeake City to Elkton and back.

Formerly Conrey's Tinsmith

ROY FOARD'S HARDWARE STORE –
The Foards started business in the former Rees' Hardware Store building. They moved to George Street about 1927.

Formerly Roy Foard's Store

WILLIE MORRIS' CHICKEN HOUSES –
On the north side of town, at the east end of Biddle Street.

HARRINGTON'S CHRYSANTHEMUM BUSINESS – George Street.

MUSHROOM HOUSE – Mt. Nebo.

BUNKER'S GARAGE AND FILLING STATION – At George and First Streets.

BUNKER'S POOL ROOM – Later run by Will Vaughan, Fred Bramble, and Ernie Fields, respectively.

MALLORY TOY'S POOL ROOM – At George and First Streets.

DAVID McCAULEY'S SOFT DRINK BUSINESS – Hemphill Street.

CHESAPEAKE BASKET CO. – North side.

BYRON BOUCHELLE'S STORE – On the east side of Bohemia Avenue between Second and Third Streets, the store sold an assortment of goods.

BUCKWORTH'S GARAGE & WHEELWRIGHT'S SHOP – On William Street (the alley between Bohemia Avenue and George Street). The building is now gone.

MASONIC HALL – Located on the Causeway, it was first a store. Later, it became the Masonic Hall, and also housed the silent movie theater and the town's post office. Jay Sager ran the reels for the movies.

JEROME "BUDDY" BIDDLE'S GARAGE – On South George Street. Mr. Biddle was a cracker-jack mechanic for Model T's.

Southern Transporation Co., at Long Creek and Back Creek, employed many people from Chesapeake City 1913-1940.
Today, Robert Dann Co. occupies the site and many of the original buildings remain intact. Photo circa 1940.

SOUTHERN TRANSPORTATION –

Located on Long Creek at the former Deibert Bros. site, this company built commercial vessels for the canal and provided the steam tugs for maneuvering them. Southern Transportation employed as many as one hundred men at one time. Some who lived on the south side of Back Creek rowed to work across the creek each day.

ADAMS' FLOATING *PLAYHOUSE* THEATER – The theater travelled the waters of the Chesapeake Bay, from Norfolk, Virginia to Chesapeake City and Port Deposit. It spent a week in Chesapeake City each summer. Townspeople have vivid memories of it and the entertainment it provided.

SLICHER'S STORE – Mr. Slicher bought the store and attached home from Henry Hager. The store, in the first block of Bohemia Avenue, specialized in boots and shoes, and was in business until the late 1940s. Mr. Slicher suffered from asthma, and frequently had to leave his customers to go outside for some fresh air to try to relieve his symtoms. He suffered many a coughing fit, according to some residents' recollections, and "of course, in those days, wasn't anything to do about asthma."

Formerly Slicer's

RIO THEATER – First run by Mr. Stubbles as a silent theatre, the theater was later bought by Mr. and Mrs. Rosen. It provided many hours of enjoyment for the townspeople. Movie tickets were 15 cents each, and the youngsters would often buy one ticket because that was all the money they could scrape together. One boy would go in and sit in the front of the theater. The rest of the boys would walk through the marsh on the canal side of the building, around to the side door, where the ticket holder would let them in after the house lights were dimmed. They saw quite a few free movies before Mr. Rosen caught on to their scheme.

BRAMBLE'S RESTAURANT AND TEA ROOM – The restaurant was in the building previously occupied by Queck's Bakery, Second Street and Bohemia Avenue. One resident recalls it as "Bramble's Restaurant, and Old Man Bramble's beer joint."

LOVETT'S STORE – The dry goods merchandise store was well-stocked, and highly regarded by the locals: "If he couldn't get it for you, it wasn't thought of yet." The store occupied the building which was previously Conrey's, in present-day Franklin Hall.

WEAVER'S GROCERY STORE – Mr. and Mrs. Harry Weaver ran this store, located on Port Herman Road. The Weavers closed the store and moved to Lancaster, Pennsylvania in 1932. There was a second store in this area, on Pepper Hill, at the south end of Port Herman Rd.

WILL BORGER'S STORE AND BUTCHER SHOP – At the corner of

George and Second Streets, the store provided groceries and meats. The building no longer stands.

THE GREAT A. & P. STORE – In the building which was once Sawtelle's, at Second Street and Bohemia Avenue.

SPA SPRINGS BOTTLING WORKS – Run by Mr. A. E. Hague, the soda-bottling business was located on south George Street. Mr. Hague sold soft drinks for 5 cents a bottle.

AMERICAN STORE – The grocery store, run by Lewis Collins and later Mr. Wilbur Needles, was at the corner of Bohemia Avenue and Second Street.

CHESAPEAKE CITY BOAT COMPANY – First launch, 1926. It was located west of town, at the end of Third Street.

NICHOLS SHOE REPAIR – In the Frank Conrey house on George Street near the Rio Theater.

JEFFERSON'S MEAT MARKET – On Biddle Street, and eventually occupied by Collins' Store.

LUPFER'S STORE – At the corner of George and Second Streets.

RIO

CHESAPEAKE CITY   Phone 2001

Fri.-Sat.   June 9-10
DIANNA BARRYMORE
Frontier Badman
—AND—
HARRIET HILLIARD
Honeymoon Lodge

Mon.-Tues.   June 12-13
Michael   Susan
O'SHEA   HAYNEARD
Jack London

Wed.-Thurs.   June 14-15
JAMES CAGNEY
Johnny Come Lately

Fri.-Sat.   June 16-17
RICHARD   DIX
The Kansan
ALSO
ADOLPH MENJOU
Hi Diddle Diddle

BUNGARD'S GENERAL STORE – At the corner of Bohemia Avenue and Third Street, across from the Methodist Church.

O'HREL'S TAILOR SHOP – Originally located next to the Rio Theater, it later moved to the foot of Bohemia Avenue.

BROWN'S LUMBER YARD – Biddle Street.

EARL WHITE'S BEER GARDEN – Bank Street.

HAROLD REYNOLDS' STORE

Formerly O'hrel's

GEORGE GORMAN'S FILLING STATION AND BLACKSMITH – Biddle Street.

TAGGART APARTMENTS – At Biddle and Hemphill Streets.

PURNER'S STORE – Cayot's Corner. General store run by William Purner. Later owned and operated by Charles Bailey.

LEWIS COLLINS' GROCERY STORE – Biddle Street.

BROWN'S LUMBER YARD – West Biddle Street, on the outskirts of town. Later became Walls Lumber Yard.

BUNKER'S GARAGE AND FILLING STATION – At George and First Streets. Later used for businesses operated by Will Vaughan, Fred Bramble, and Ernie Fields.

DOLPH WHARTON'S BEER GARDEN – At the corner of Basil Avenue and Randalia Road.

DELMAR CURRY'S SANDWICH SHOP – On Bohemia Avenue between Lovett's Store and the American Store.

KIBLER'S BOARDING HOUSE – In the third block of Bohemia Avenue.

MEWHITER'S DRUG STORE – At Bohemia Avenue and First Street.

WOOLEYHAN TRUCKING COMPANY – Located on West Biddle Street, the company hauled freight from the canal night boats to Wilmington, Delaware.

Formerly Bob Foard's Store

BOB FOARD'S STORE – An "all-around" general store located at "Churchtown," the intersection of St. Augustine and Cayot's Corner Roads.

SAGER'S CHICKEN HOUSES – On South George Street.

LOSTEN'S DAIRY – North side, east of town.

Business Ads from an 1877 map:

"Blacksmiths:

James Warner, General Blacksmith - carriages repaired, horse shoeing done in best order, etc. etc. etc.

Jacob Metz, Blacksmith and Carriage maker is skillful in his profession and warrants his work. Horse-shoeing and job work done to order.

Druggists:

T.B. Hopper, Druggist and Pharmaceutist, Dealer in Drugs, Medicines, Paints, Oils, Dye Stuffs, Fancy Goods, Perfumery, etc. Particular attention given to compounding Physicians' prescriptions.

B.J. Williams, Dealer in Drugs, Patent Medicines, Chemicals, Fancy and Toilet articles, Brushes, Perfumery, Paints, Glass, etc.

Hotels:

Capt. Firman Layman, Proprietor of Bayard House. First class accomodations for Man and Beast.

M.L. Realy, Proprietor of Chesapeake House. A first-class Hotel in all its appointments. Choice Wines, Liquors, Ales, Cigars, etc. constantly on hand. Prime salt water oysters served in every style in season."

ASCO - The American Stores Co., 1926

ASCO - The American Stores Co., 1932

The American Stores Co. (1946)

Photo courtesy of Betty Needles Watson

ABOVE: American Store employees pose in front of the store in 1946. Left to right: Betty Needles, Tillie Blendy, Kathleen DeShane, Olive Spear, Anna Merchant, Dorothy Downs, Wilbur Needles, Walter Bennett, American Stores Superintendent Harry Porter, and Hazel Hessey.

OPPOSITE PAGE TOP: The American Store, 1926, at the foot of Bohemia Avenue next to Franklin Hall. Shown are Mark Alcorn (left) and Lewis Collins, Sr. This building is no longer standing.

OPPOSITE PAGE BOTTOM: The American Store, 1932, at the corner of Bohemia Avenue and Second Street. Left to right: John Dwyer, Frank Bristow, and Miss Nellie Reid.

OFTEN HEARD
AROUND
CHESAPEAKE
CITY:

"ASCO beans make ASCO boom"

1924 "Charles P. West died at Back Creek at the home of his nephew R.B. Lake. He was a widower and was 82. He was the sexton and superintendent at Bethel Church and cemetery for many years. He was a veteran of the Civil War."

1924 "Leonard Schrader, aged 19 years, son of Mr. and Mrs. George Schrader of Summit Bridge, Delaware was drowned Tuesday while working on the dredging operation on the canal near his home."

1932 "Mr. and Mrs. Henry Hager left for Miami, Florida, for a well-earned vacation, the first in their 35 years of married life."

1931 "Mr. William E. Briscoe, Town Point, left for Annapolis, Maryland. Mr. Briscoe is a recently elected member of the House of Representatives."

1931 "A beautiful night-blooming cereus at the home of Mrs. Andrew Slicher was much admired last Saturday night. The plant had seven perfect blooms."

1920 "Town Point fishermen of gill nets and haul nets are getting ready for the season. William T. Broadwater and son are the only ones left doing pound fishing on a larger scale this season."

DR. D. SMITHERS
Dentist
Chesapeake City, Md.

1930 "The many people who like homemade clothes will be glad to know that Mrs. Fred Ginn has taken up the work. With the departure of our old standbys, there has been a dearth of dressmakers in our town."

1900 "Mule team drivers earn $21 per month. There is a stable at each end of the canal, and drivers can stay over-night in quarters connected to the stable."

1928 "A number of sleighs were seen on our streets for the first time in a number of years."

1925 "A high tension wire broke and fell on low tension ones on the north side, at the home of J.R. Loveless. The heat was so intense, the legs were melted off the electric washing machine."

A. OHREL
Cleaning, Pressing
& Repairing
Chesapeake City, Md.

1931 "According to a Wilmington paper, the sale of Town Point Wharf to Mr. Frank R. Jones has been effected. Mr. Jones will convert the property into an amusement park and will erect several bungalows."

1930 "A Mr. Ward, who conducts a travelling medicine show, has purchased a tract of land on Mr. Nebo and will erect a dwelling thereon."

1920 "Everybody has a garden."

1930 "Mr. Mallory Toy who purchased the Wooley homestead has sold the boxwood on the lawn for $1500.00 and it is now being removed for transplanting on one of the duPont estates."

1927 "The Dr. Smithers farm, near Bohemia Bridge, has been sold to Senator Thomas Bayard of Delaware, for an undisclosed sum."

1877 "Some graceless wretch placed two pieces of timber across the board walk near Masonic Hall the other night, in such a way as to seriously endanger life and limb. Whoever did the deed is unworthy to live in a decent community."

1877 "One of the Institutions of Chesapeake City is Brooks' Marble Works, on Chesapeake Street, nearly opposite the Chesapeake House. Mr William Brooks, the chief of the establishment is one of the most accomplished workers in marble in the State, and is therefore fully competent to execute any order placed in his hands---from a costly monument to the most delicate parlor ornament."

1877 "Foot-ball, quoits, jumping matches, marbles, and hoop rolling are now rife in Chesapeake City. Kite flying will no doubt soon begin."

"All us fellows went down to the Adams' Floating Theater one night to see a demonstration of some man breaking a big rock over a man's chest with a sledge hammer. We got the idea to try it ourselves, so the next day we found a big rock and a sledge and set about to do it. Just about time we got ready, we all chickened out. Good thing, too."

– Chesapeake City resident

The Adams' Floating Theatre

uilt in Washington, North Carolina in 1914, the Adams' Floating Theatre was officially registered as *Playhouse* in its hailing port of Baltimore, Maryland. It was 128 feet long, 34 feet in beam, and drew only 14 inches of water. It could seat 700 people in the auditorium, boxes and balcony, with 8 dressing rooms behind the 19 foot-wide stage. Additional rooms, including a dining room, were located forward. The theater was built, owned, and operated by James Adams and his wife, who were former circus performers. It was towed by the powerboats *Elk* and *Trouper*.

The *Playhouse* was destroyed by fire on the Savannah River in Georgia in 1941.

Mr. and Mrs Adams built a home in Chesapeake City on Mt. Nebo.

DID YOU KNOW?

In 1924, Edna Ferber spent a week on Adams' Floating Theatre collecting material for her novel *Show Boat*. After the book won popular acclaim, the owners of the *Playhouse* felt they would benefit from some of the publicity given the novel. The vessel's sign was removed and "The Original Floating Theatre" was painted on either side in letters three feet high.

Town Government

1876

Commissioners: ....DAVID PALMER
DR. J. V. WALLACE
T. B. HOPPER
J. A. BOULDEN
JAMES CUMMINS

Town Bailiff: ....N. A. COLMARY

Constable: ....G. R. CARPENTER

Postmaster: ....A. P. BARWICK

Magistrate: ....G. F. CHRISFIELD

RESIDENT OFFICIALS OF THE
CHESAPEAKE & DELAWARE CANAL COMPANY

Superintendent: ....JOHN R. PRICE

Asst. Superintendent: ....J. F. PRICE

Collector: ....J. T. HEDRICK

1st Asst. Collector: ....T. J. CLEAVER

2nd Asst. Collector: ....W. SMITHERS

Master Carpenter: ....D. PALMER

Chief Engineer: ....T. LORRAINE

1st Asst. Engineer: ......SAM'L POWELL

2nd Asst. Engineer: ......J. W. HARRIOTT

From the *Chesapeake Chesapike* newspaper – circa 1876

"Apples – Get Your Apples!"

"Alfred, the huckster, came through town with fresh fruits and vegetables on his wagon every summer for quite a few years. Could only get fresh items when it was their growin' season around here. Only time we ever saw an orange was at Christmastime. It was quite a treat."

– Chesapeake City resident

Schools, & Churches

Organizations

Miss Katie Loveless' Class, 1918

Schools

The older citizens of Chesapeake City in the early 1900s, not unlike those in many small communities of the time, shared experiences and know-how with those coming along behind them. They had grown up in an era when formal schooling was in its infancy. In spite of that, many could "read and figure plenty well enough to get along." Their wealth of knowledge came from life experience. When the older residents of today speak about growing up in the early 1900s, they speak with pride in their accomplishments and regard for people who influenced them in their younger years. These residents benefited from both the traditional education passed along by their

High School, Chesapeake City, Md.

Photo courtesy of Mr. & Mrs. John Sager

Postcard of Chesapeake City High School in 1910. The school was built in 1886 on the south side of Third Street, just a few steps beyond the sidewalk.

elders and the earliest formal county school system.

Lack of transportation precluded centralized schools; rural schools dotted the landscape. As recently as 1920, the Chesapeake City area had eight one-room schoolhouses. There were two schools in town as well: one for white children and one for black children.

The one-room schools in the rural areas covered all grades. Teachers often moved from one school to another – perhaps to a different area – but were well-remembered by those who attended the schools. It seems from the collective memory of today's citizens, nearly all "could put a kid in his place in short order, wasn't no fooling around, except of course for an occasional child who was downright contemptible, and that one usually ended up quitting."

Although part of an organized system, each rural school took on its own character. Most of the one-room schools in the Chesapeake City area closed by 1923 when a centralized school system was adopted. The one-room "coloured schools" did not close until 1941 when all black children were centrally schooled in Elkton.

NEWS FLASH

"The Hog Growers Association of Cecil County, 2nd district, organized at a meeting at Cayot's Corner Schoolhouse."

– Cecil County News, 1918

DID YOU KNOW?

A park on the north side of Chesapeake City was named *Helen Titter Park,* for a beloved teacher who taught her whole career at Chesapeake City School. She taught many town residents and their children from 1929 until the 1960s.

CHESAPEAKE CITY SCHOOL

Today's Chesapeake City Elementary School occupies the 1940 building.

The Chesapeake City School, on the south side of town, was built in 1886 at a cost of $5000. At one time it had a front entranceway complete with a bell tower (See photo on page 121). In 1890, the school was enlarged and the bell tower removed. Another section was added about 1920 to accomodate additional students when the one-room schools began closing.

That school building served Chesapeake City until 1940, when the present building was erected behind the original. The old one was demolished, and a sweeping green lawn now extends from the street to the front of the more recent school building.

In 1959, after the completion of the new first district high school, the Chesapeake City School housed elementary grades only. In the 1990s, the school expanded again to accomodate more students. Today, it houses kindergarten through fifth grade.

ST. AUGUSTINE SCHOOL, No. 2

The school was located just east of St. Augustine Church, with the foundation dating to 1850. A new school building was erected at the same site in 1880 by John Conrey, for $488. On average, twelve to fifteen pupils attended the school. Drinking water was brought in twice weekly from a nearby farm. In 1910, the trustees were Mrs. Charles Ellison, Robert B. Ford, and Mrs. Myrtle E. Wilson.

CAYOT'S CORNER SCHOOL, No. 3

Located about three miles south of Chesapeake City, the school occupied a lot purchased in 1886 from the adjacent Methodist Church. The school averaged twelve to fifteen pupils. Two of today's area residents recall attending school at Cayot's Corner, and playing ball in the school yard.

Photo courtesy of Janet Titter

TOWN POINT SCHOOL, No. 4

The school was built in 1859 on Port Herman Road by the Jackson Bros. for $420. It occupied a lot bought from Joshua Clayton for $50.

Each child had his own agate drinking cup, and each morning, one of the children would fetch a bucket of water from a spring across the road. When it snowed, the children in this school had the privilege of sledding down Pepper Hill during their recess time.

In 1923, the trustees were Howard Pyle, William Fears, and Clarence Broadwater.

Since the school closed, the building has been converted to a private residence.

Photo courtesy of Debbie Lovejoy

Town Point School as a single room frame building in 1900 (left); and today, a completely restored cottage home overlooking Port Herman and the Elk River.

DID YOU KNOW?

In 1931 Miss Katie G. Loveless, teacher of the primary grade in Chesapeake City school, wrote the play entitled "Mother Goose's Party," and sold the publication rights to a Baltimore publishing company.

CHESAPEAKE CITY SCHOOL, No. 5

In 1851, a one-room school was held in the Trinity Methodist Church building. In 1854, the "Academy" was built at the corner of Biddle and Hemphill Streets, on the north side of town. It had two stories, with a classroom on each floor. After the new school was built in town, the Academy housed only the first three grades, and was finally shut down in 1913.

PIVOT SCHOOL, No. 6

Named after the bridge which crossed the C & D Canal at Bethel, the original schoolhouse was near the site of Bethel Methodist Church. The earliest school at Bethel, Thompson's School, was in place in 1772. In 1882, a new school was erected by the Jackson Brothers at a cost of $700. It was located in a wooded area near Bethel Cemetery.

The trustees in 1910 were Mrs. Tabitha Thornton, Mr. Henry George, and Mr. Charles Kirk.

The school no longer stands.

BACK CREEK NECK SCHOOL, No. 8

Located on the road to Welch Point, the school lot contained 76 perches of land (approximately 1/2 acre) by deed. The school's date of construction is unknown. Built of rough-hewn logs in a grove of pine trees, the school acquired the nickname "Pine Tree College." Eventually, the outside was weather-boarded and the inside walls were plastered. A nearby stream supplied water for the school. This building burned in 1915, and a new school was built by J. Frank Simpers at a cost of $394. It opened just three months after the first burned. An average of eighteen to twenty pupils attended. The school closed in 1918, and the building was sold to Locust Point farmer Taylor McKenney.

CHESAPEAKE CITY COLOURED SCHOOL

The school was established in 1869 on Pine Street in Chesapeake City. Fifteen to twenty children attended under the tutelage of Miss Emma Boyer. The school was closed in 1941, after which all Cecil County coloured children attended school in Elkton. The building is a private home today.

CONCORD COLOURED SCHOOL

The school opened in the 1860s in the small settlement of Concord, south of Chesapeake City. Twenty to thirty children attended. Miss Laura Haskins was the schoolmarm. She often walked to school from Town Point Neck, about three miles away.

Teachers in the Chesapeake City area - 1875 to 1930

Stella Bishop (Cayot's Corner)

Helen Davidson (Cayot's Corner)

Emma Haller (Cayot's Corner), 1918

Katie Loveless (Cayot's Corner), 1917

Anna Luthinger (Cayot's Corner)

Clara McCoy (Cayot's Corner)

Elizabeth Satterfield (Cayot's Corner)

Myrtle Templeman (Cayot's Corner)

Charlotte Warner (Cayot's Corner), 1907

Lula Brown (Town Point School)

Lula Bryson (Town Point School)

Ella Cannan (Town Point School), 1910

John Cavender (Town Point School), 1875

Alice Hager (Town Point School), 1923

Laura Jones (Town Point School)

Arrie McCoy (Town Point School)

Gertrude Manlove (Town Point School), 1922

Sadie Nichol (Town Point School)

Ima Taylor (Town Point School), 1914

Mary Walter (Town Point School)

Emma Willis (Town Point School)

Carrie Wright (Town Point School)

Sarah Cavenaugh (Back Creek Neck)

Flora Davis (Back Creek Neck)

Augusta Egee (Back Creek Neck), 1915

Mary Millburn (Back Creek Neck)

Jennie Packard (Back Creek Neck)

Belle Price (Back Creek Neck)

Lottie Warner (Back Creek Neck)

Mattie Warner (Back Creek Neck)

Mamie Black (Pivot School)

Anna Buckworth (Pivot School), 1902

Mary Fillingame (Pivot School), 1925

Maggie Jenness (Pivot School), 1888

Sadie Nichol (Pivot School)

Marguerite Potts (Pivot School), 1919

Carmen Price (Pivot School), 1926

Ida Staples (Pivot School), 1878

Lelia Thornton (Pivot School), 1910

Millie Walmsley (Pivot School), 1894

Stella Bishop (St. Augustine School), 1910

Ada Davis (St. Augustine School)

Eva Dean (St. Augustine School), 1902

Arrie Duhamell (St. Augustine School), 1894

Addie Ford (St. Augustine School), 1876

Evelyn Kibler (St. Augustine School)

Helen Larazalere (St. Augustine School), 1899

Katie Loveless (St. Augustine School), 1917

Clara McCoy (St. Augustine School), 1881

Ethel Vineyard (St. Augustine School), 1901

Miriam Biddle (Chesapeake City School)

Ruth Biddle (Chesapeake City School)

Mae Buckworth (Chesapeake City School)

Mildred Carnes (Chesapeake City School)

Mary Cooper (Chesapeake City School)

Helen Green (Chesapeake City School)

Alice Hager (Chesapeake City School)

Katie Loveless (Chesapeake City School)

Louise McCauley (Chesapeake City School)

Mae McFadden (Chesapeake City School)

Miss Mower (Chesapeake City School)

Sadie Nichol (Chesapeake City School)

Quebie Nye (Chesapeake City School)

Helen Titter (Chesapeake City School)

Mary Walter (Chesapeake City School)

Laura Haskins (Concord Coloured School)

Emma Boyer (Ches. City Coloured School)

Cayot's Corner School, 1920

FRONT ROW: Albert Buckworth, Benny Ross, Charles Price. MIDDLE ROW: unknown, Ralph Pyle, unknown, Anna Pyle (Ralph's sister), Edgar Ross, Miss Anna Luthringer (teacher), Clark Buckworth. BACK ROW: Mildred Whiteoak, unknown, unknown, Russell Cleaver.

1946 Chesapeake City Graduating Class

Photo courtesy of Roland "Flint" Sheldon

FIRST ROW: John Reynolds, Borno Green, Walter "Bud" Carlton, Cliff Ginn. SECOND ROW: Roland "Flint" Sheldon, George Pierce, Gene Robinson, Robert Foard, George Yedinak. THIRD ROW: Annie Haggerty, Mildred Maksyn, Jayne McCommons, Magdalene Kutz. FOURTH ROW: Jean McConnell, Catherine Ann Beaston, Winifred Manlove, Elizabeth Crowgey (teacher), Virginia Harasymtzuk, Ramona Spear, Shirley Spear.

Ball Teams

Chesapeake City High School

1924 Soccer Champs

Photo courtesy of Morrison Watson

FRONT ROW: John Wilson, Willard McCauley, Raymond Whiteoak (captain), Burton Wilson, Franklin Whiteoak.
MIDDLE ROW: Edgar Pensel, Marvin Savin, Frank Bristow, John Walter. BACK ROW: Howard March, Melvin Lum, Pete Waclawski, Ralph Hazel, Guy Johnson (principal & coach).

Town Baseball Team, circa 1925

FRONT ROW:
unknown
unknown
Alfred "Nip" Pierce
Charles Elllison

MIDDLE ROW:
John Schaefer
Herb Watson
unknown
Henry Borger
Parker Noland

BACK ROW:
"Punch" Harriott
Edwin Stapp
Ralph Watson
Tom Savin
Bill Vaughan

Photo courtesy of Morrison Watson

1928 Chesapeake City School Baseball Team

Austin Ginn
Frank Bristoe
Noble Benson
Michael Hernick
Frankie Stevens
Alex Yedinak
Earl "Jazz" Morgan
Clayton Brooks
Jimmy Peaper
Alan Ginn
John Sager
Sydney "Shine" Crawford

Photo courtesy of Mr. & Mrs. John Sager

1931 & 1932 Soccer Team

The 1931 and 1932 Chesapeake City High School Eastern Shore Championship Soccer Team

FRONT ROW:
Mr. MacBride (principal)
Jack Harrison
Roger Watkins
Morris Kane
Buzz Watson
Frank Boyko
Buss Wharton
Allen Ginn

MIDDLE ROW:
Reds Eveland
Perry Hevern
Herb Watson

BACK ROW:
Ed Losten
Herb Edmunds
Burke Bramble
Allen Benson

Photo courtesy of Morrison Watson

Chesapeake City High School

1935 Volleyball Team

FRONT ROW:
Virginia Lloyd

MIDDLE ROW:
unknown
Stella Maksyn
Alice Marie Davis

BACK ROW:
Ruth Crawford
Sophie Harasymtzuk
Helen Bailey
Lucy Fillingame
Katie Tycki
Vera Gagnon
Anna Yedinak

Photo courtesy of Lucy F. Titter

1946 Soccer Team

Winners of the Cecil County High School Championship against Calvert High School. Score:12-4

From Chesapeake City High School Yearbook, courtesy of Roland "Flint" Sheldon

FRONT ROW:
John Thornton
Melvin Lum
Mike Losten
Harold Reynolds
George Pierce
Walter Carlton
Rodney Dixon
Clifton Ginn
MIDDLE ROW:
Marshall McCommons
Charles Sheldon
Richard Caleb
Pete Tereszcuk
Nick Boyko
Frank Sheldon
Billy Luzetsky
Carey Birch
Galen Reynolds
BACK ROW:
Robert Foard
Borno Green
George Yedinak

1950 Town Soccer Team

Photo courtesy of Roland "Flint" Sheldon

FRONT ROW:
Norman Hessey
Bill Trush
Billy Luzetsky
Sam Bramble
Earl Harmer
MIDDLE ROW:
Jule Bristow
Maurice Hudson
George Beaston
Wallace Hudson
Jimmy Kirk
BACK ROW:
Donnie Preston
"Baldy" Thornton
Harry Austin
Charlie Noland
Jack Kinter
Frank Bristow
Cliff Preston
Referee (unknown).

VOL. II. NO. 2.   CHESAPEAKE CITY, MD.   MARCH, 1929

THE "WHY" OF CLUBS

The term "extra-curricular activities" is coming to be used for those activities which more and more are to be found in the better-type progressive high schools of today. It refers to projects which, although carried on under the direction of the school and sponsored by some teacher, are nevertheless not regular classroom work. Athletics are one very important unit. The old "literary society", now fast disappearing, was another important step. It is being succeeded by various other organizations often known as clubs.

People ignorant of the real reason for these growing activities often thoughtlessly make the statement that the schools are for learning and not for amusement. Granted. But does a thing have to be unpleasant to cause learning? Can not a person do a thing for the sheer pleasure of doing something and at the same time benefit? The answer is obvious. Pupils often learn far more outside the classroom than they do in it.

Clubs are being formed to give everyone a chance to follow out some hobby or particular interest. Every person should have some hobby. One very eminent authority says that the number of varied interests a man has determines the amount and extent of his education. High School clubs give pupils a chance to learn things not by merely reading about them, but by actually doing them. They are practical, not theoretical. And so we formed Glee Clubs for those interested in music; a craftsmanship club for those who like to "make things"; an aviation club for those interested in that extremely absorbing subject; a home arts club for those interested in making the home a better place to live in; and a science club for carrying out interesting experiments.

Clubs should be, and are, run by

(Continued on Page 3)

HOME ARTS CLUB

The first meeting of the Home Arts Club, a club for furthering interest in the home, was held January 10. The following officers were elected: Madalyn Benson, Hostess; Eloise Howard, Assist. Hostess; Gladys Dean, Sec.-Treas.; Mrs. Sherman, Faculty Adviser.

It was decided to have meetings the first and third Monday evenings of each month. At the second meeting of the club a table was set correctly. The members then left room while the table was set incorrectly. Catherine Lishowid received a printed towel to embroider for finding the most mistakes. At the third meeting the girls brought something to sew. Those that didn't bring anything to sew looked at magazines and played games. The last meeting was held February 4. Several short talks were given on the home.

The latest and biggest project to be undertaken by the Club is the changing of the now unused former manual training room into a club room. This will be used by all the clubs, but the initiative is being taken by the Home Arts Club.

SCIENCE CLUB

Science is one of the most attractive fields in modern learning. Many of the students of this school interested in experimenting in some of the things in Science have decided to form themselves into a Science Club. The first meeting was held for suggestions as to what the members would like to experiment with. Paul Hrynick was elected president. A second meeting was held of late and we are getting ready now for some experiments. Chemistry, electricity, and astronomy are some of the things we are taking up. The Science Club now promises to be one of the most prosperous in the school. Miss Farmer is sponsoring the club.

SCHOOL GROUND IMPROVEMENT LAUNCHED

Those who pass the school occasionally can readily notice that our school *ground is very unattractive. Some* of those who realize this are doing their best to make improvements. The Parent Teachers Association formed a committee to solicit different parts of the town. The committee is as follows:

Mrs. J. Glesner Brooks, Chairman Mrs. Ralph Watson, Mrs. Jay Sager, Mrs. Earl Sykes, Mrs. Ward Beaston, Miss Florence Egee, Mrs. Foster, Miss Wilda McCauley, Mrs. Nelson Cooling, Mrs. Fowler, Mrs. Ireland, Mrs. Noble Benson.

The high school students made some very striking posters and put them around in different prominent places. They also assisted in distributing publicity leaflets.

With the money that is donated shubbery is to be bought and planted; the front yard planted as a lawn, and if the money warrants, playground equipment such as swings and see-saws, etc. will be provided for the children. The solicitors have reported once, and about $90 has been contributed. That seems to be a fair starting and those who haven't given a liberal amount are urged to give now and help this community project. Don't wait to be asked. Any of the collectors will be glad to receive the money. Several people have already shown a fine spirit by contributing even before being asked to do so.

AVIATION CLUB

As many of the students are interested in Aviation a club has been formed to study different types of airplanes and build model ones. The first meeting was held February 18. Mr. Hawkins gave an introductory talk on aviation and Herbert Edmonds was elected chairman. A committee was formed to find some interesting

Continued on fourth page

EXCURSIONS OF THE PHYSICS CLASS

The physics class went on board the Dredge "Florida", instead of doing laboratory work on January 28th. The object of the trip was to see what application of physical principles was made. Through the courtesy of the captain of the dredge, the trip was made both interesting and instructive. It was interesting to learn that the oil, which was burned to run the steam engines, was heated before being used, in order that oxidation might take place more rapidly. The large steam engines are used to run a large cutter which goes back and forth across the canal bed, cutting and loosening the soil, preparing it for the centrifugal pump which forces the mixture of soil and water through the long pipe line to the reservation, or as commonly known, "the dump".

On February 5th the class went to Conowingo to see the Power plant. The guide was courteous enough to explain how the turbines were installed and how they are used to drive the dynamos or generators. He showed us the central room and explained how necessary it is that the workers there be careful in controlling the machinery. He explained that, as less power is needed during some parts of the day, some turbines are not used all the time. He pointed out the transformers that are used to step up the voltage in order that a high voltage may be transmitted to Philadelphia because it is more economical.

CRAFTSMANSHIP CLUB

The Craftsmanship Club, as its name indicates, is composed of students who enjoy working with tools, "making things." Allen Robson was elected chairman at the first meeting and has been persistent in going ahead on the first project—a good-sized model of Columbus' flag ship

(Continued on page four.)

In 1929, Chesapeake City School's newspaper sported a masthead featuring the Chesapeake City Lift Bridge with the initials CCHS.

Courtesy of Lucy Titter

Bethel Cemetery, 1960

Churches

I n the 1600s, when settlement began on the Eastern Shore, church parishes served as the focal points around which communities grew. A variety of religious denominations were represented in this area. Although Chesapeake City has never boasted a population greater than 2500, as many as eleven churches have served the town and its environs.

BETHEL METHODIST EPISCOPAL CHURCH

Situated on the south side of the C & D Canal, two miles east of Chesapeake City, this church was organized in 1771 by Richard Wright. It was the second oldest Methodist Church on the Delmarva Peninsula. The first church building was erected in 1780. The second church was built of brick in 1849. Some of the older residents in Chesapeake City recall attending Sunday School in the church. After the bridge at Bethel was eliminated, the area dwindled drastically in population until only a few families occupied the settlement. Eventually the church was no longer used and was abandoned by its affiliated Methodist Conference. In the early 1960s, it was demolished by the U.S. Army Corps of Engineers during the canal-widening project. Bethel Church hosted a contemporary of John Wesley as one of its first speakers.

Photo courtesy of U.S. Army Corps of Engineers

ABOVE: Bethel Church, circa 1960.

RIGHT: Bethel Cemetery entrance gate, circa 1870.

Photo courtesy of Morrison Watson

BETHEL METHODIST EPISCOPAL CHURCH

ABOVE: Bethel Church as it appeared in 1900.

BELOW: The sanctuary of Bethel Church in 1900.

Bethel Church's founding congregation, circa 1772, worshipped in Thompson's School before the church was built. In 1790, Bethel Chapel was built, and it was rebuilt again in 1849. Following is a list of pastors of Bethel Church, 1875-1936.

George R. Bristor 1875-1877

Lucius C. Matlock 1877-1879

E.C. Atkins 1884-1886

J.T. Van Burkelow 1886-1887

Asbury Burke 1887-1889

H.E. Gardner 1889-1891

Wilmer Joggard 1891-1892

George W. Bowman 1892-1893

Thomas B. Hunter 1893-1896

William H. Benford 1896-1898

George S. Conoway 1898-1901

George W. Dawson.............1901-1903

Edward H. Collins 1903-1904

Edward K. Creed ....1904(died)

William P. Taylor 1904-1907

John M. Lindale 1907-1911

Asbury Burke 1911-1914

J. H. Wilson 1914-1918

J.H. Geoghegan 1919-1924

C.D. Sharples 1924-1931

J. B. Vaughn 1931-1936

BETHEL CHURCH CEMETERY

Photo courtesy of U.S. Army Corps of Engineers

Disinterment of remains at Bethel Cemetery in 1963 by workers of Tyson F. Sartin, Inc., St. Georges, Delaware.

In 1963, a large portion of Bethel Cemetery was relocated to make way for the widening of the C & D Canal, under the direction of the U.S. Army Corps of Engineers. More than 1100 graves were removed to an area just south of the cemetery. Many were unidentified. One known grave was that of Gov. Clayton of Delaware.

When reinterment was completed, the Bethel Methodist Episcopal Church was demolished, and an integral part of Methodist history was lost. All that remains is an historical marker at the site.

TOWN POINT UNITED METHODIST CHURCH

The original church, in the village of Port Herman, was built and dedicated in 1917, free and clear of debt. The Fears family of Port Herman was instrumental in keeping the church viable during the early 1900s. As the Town Point population began to swell during the 1970s, it outgrew the little church on Cherry Street. The church still had no bathroom facilities or running water.

In the 1980s, the church was granted a two-acre parcel about halfway up Port Herman Road from the village. The parishoners considered moving the old church, but instead decided to build a new one. A fellowship hall was constructed first in the early 1980s. A few years later a new sanctuary

Photo courtesy of Mary Anna Taylor

Town Point M. E. Church in 1917, shortly after construction.

was added. The lovely white country church on Port Herman Road today is a testament to the tenacity of this rural congregation. The original church building is now a private home.

Town Point United Methodist Church, 2000.

ST. BASIL'S UKRANIAN CATHOLIC CHURCH

A large contingent of Ukranian people arrived in Chesapeake City in 1910. They built the quaint little church atop the hill on Basil Avenue, just south of town, in 1920. The land for the church was donated by the Wasylczuk family. St. Basil's opened an orphange and a nunnery on the north side. The orphange is no longer in operation.

ST. ROSE OF LIMA CATHOLIC CHURCH

The St. Rose of Lima parish formed in the 1860s of mostly German immigrants. They met in private homes until 1874, when land was purchased for a church building. People came by steamship to celebrate the dedication of the new church. The brick church still stands on a hill on the north side of town. Route 213 bisects the church's property today.

BETHEL A. M. E. CHURCH

This church, on Second and Charles Streets in South Chesapeake City, has been a center for African American worship since 1873. Its architecture is similar to that of the Presbyterian church on the north side of town.

BETHESDA METHODIST – CAYOT'S CORNER

About three hundred yards east of the present-day intersection of Routes 213 and 310, three miles south of Chesapeake City, a small church served the rural farming population. It began circa 1772 as a log cabin. Ralph and Anna Pyle recall attending Sunday School at this site, circa 1915-1920. Land for the Cayot's Corner School, adjacent to the church and graveyard, was purchased from this church. One tombstone still stands today, and is the only remaining marker of the site.

NEWS FLASH

"Passengers numbering four hundred which boarded the steamer Lancaster in Port Deposit and Havre de Grace, arrived in Chesapeake City and walked up the hill to dedicate the new St. Rose's Parish church."

– *Cecil Democrat,*
1875

TRINITY UNITED METHODIST CHURCH

Trinity Church began as a Methodist church group that gathered in the home of Mrs. Cropper, at the corner of Bohemia Avenue and First Street. When the group outgrew the home meetings in the 1830s, it held its services in a rented schoolhouse. In 1846, land was purchased along Third Street, between Bohemia Avenue and George Street, and a frame building was soon completed. This first frame building was rented out in its early years and also used as a school for the town. The congregation eventually outgrew the building, which then was torn down. In 1889, the church was rebuilt of Port Deposit granite, and this building remains in use today. There was an adjacent cemetery until 1958, when the cemetery was excavated to make room for the present fellowship hall. This church and Town Point Church together form the Chesapeake City Methodist parish.

Photo courtesy of Mr. & Mrs. John Sager

ABOVE: The Trinity Methodist Church in South Chesapeake City began as a wooden clapboard structure in the late 1800s. FACING PAGE, TOP: Trinity Church postcard, circa 1919. Note the gas streetlight in the foreground and the porch overhang from what was once Bungard's Store on the corner of Bohemia Avenue and Third Street. FACING PAGE, BOTTOM: Trinity Church today.

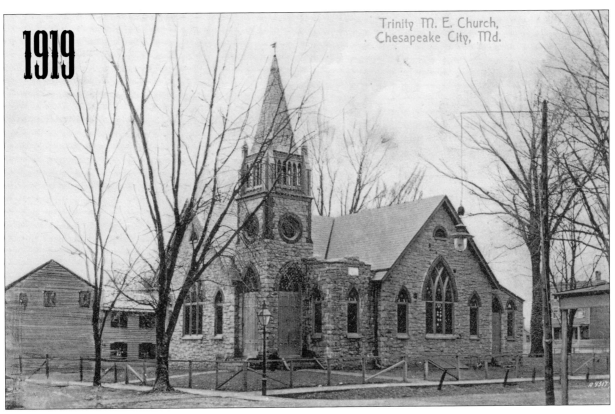

1919

Trinity M. E. Church, Chesapeake City, Md.

2000

∞ 145 ∞

FIRST PRESBYTERIAN CHURCH

The church has served the town since 1860. Located on Biddle Street on the north side of Chesapeake City, the origianl 32- x 50-foot sanctuary with furnishings was built in 1858 at a cost of $2500. Presbyterianism took hold in this area circa 1723 near Bethel, on the shores of Broad Creek, with a congregation under the guidance of Richard Thompson.

EBENEEZER A. M. E. CHURCH

This church, located on Route 310 about three miles south of Chesapeake City, is now encompassed by Mrs. Richard C. duPont's estate. It was built about 1855. Mr. Harry Jackson, a carpenter from Chesapeake City, added the front vestibule.

ST. AUGUSTINE EPISCOPAL CHURCH

Situated in the area known as Churchtown, three miles east of Route 213 on Route 310, this picturesque little church had its beginnings in the 1700s. The present structure was built in the mid-1800s and has been serving the area ever since. A unique Austrian pipe organ with a reverse-color keyboard graces the sanctuary. The adjacent cemetery includes such area surnames as Foard, Hynson, Broadwater, and Mears.

THE CHURCH OF THE GOOD SHEPHERD

The affiliate church of St. Augustine Parish, Good Shepherd is on George Street in South Chesapeake City and has an adjacent parish house. The church was built about 1883, and now shares Sunday morning worship duties with St. Augustine.

Good Shepherd parish hall

Fire Company

VOLUNTEER FIRE CO. NO. 1 OF CHESAPEAKE CITY, INC.

Around midnight on March 16, 1911, the people of Chesapeake City were called from their homes by a fire alarm. The town did not have a fire company and the residents had to use buckets of water to douse the fire. The fire was located on Canal Street, on the north side of town. The men were doing all they could do to put an end to the blaze, but it had too much of a head start.

The steamer *Penn* was going through the Canal at the time, and the captain, seeing the blaze, stopped the boat to help. Some buildings were saved, but not before the fire destroyed three homes.

The people of the town hastened to organize a fire company, and a meeting was held on April 1, 1911 in a building owned by Mr. Reed. At this meeting they decided to ask each taxpayer in the town to pay a certain amount to finance the fire company.

Subscriptions taken from the townspeople amounted to $600.10. On April 13th at Mr. Reed's store, the fire company was organized and administrative officers were appointed to serve a three month term.

At the next meeting, the administrators approved a set of by-laws and agreed to call in the list when the subscriptions reached $900. Dues were set at $1.00. At this same meeting the company was officially named Volunteer Fire Company No. 1 of Chesapeake City.

In May 1911, a committee was appointed to buy an engine. This committee went to William B. Hargraves, Secretary and Treasurer of Building and Wrecking Company of Baltimore, who purchased a First Class-make fire engine steamer of the suction type that had been used in a theatrical play called "Fighting The Flames." The cost of the engine was $366.30. This was a great bargain, as the engine was

NEWS FLASH

"Milton Lloyd, son of Mr. & Mrs. Joseph Lloyd, narrowly escaped drowning on Saturday, when he fell into the locks. The little fellow was rescued by James Kane."

– *Cecil County News*, January 28, 1920

⨯ 148 ⨯

nearly new.

After the engine was purchased, the company bought a suction hose for $100 and 1600 feet of hose for $1200. The length of hose reached from Back Creek or the canal to any house in town. In those days, self-propelled equipment had not been invented, and the firemen had to pull the steamer wherever it was needed to fight the fires.

W. A. Queck, G. N. Bennett, and J. P. Steele formed a building committee to find a suitable place to house the fire engine. The committee decided to rent a building (formerly a butcher shop and pool room) for both housing the engine and holding meetings. The company proceeded to acquire other necessary equipment such as hose carts, lanterns, ladders and axes.

TOP RIGHT: 1950 firehouse at Chesapeake City.

BOTTOM RIGHT: Firehouse as it appears today with the 1965 addition.

FAR RIGHT: First firehouse, built in 1911 on the Causeway; it is now located on the north side of town.

In the early days, residents alerted the firemen to fires by ringing all the church bells in town. Later, alarms were sounded by the Canal and Back Creek Towing Company, using the whistle on the lock engine. About 1913, the firemen began using a steel locomotive rim to sound the alarm. The code was four short blasts for fires on the north side, and one long and two short blasts for fires on the south side.

Midway through 1911, the U.S. government offered to lease to the fire company a parcel of ground on the Causeway. The building committee accepted the offer, and set the

Photo courtesy of Morrison Watson

Elizabeth Wells Taylor poses astride Chesapeake City's fire alarm, an improvised locomotive rim, which was located on the wall of the canal lock, circa 1925.

A vintage triple combination (hose, chemical, and pumper from the early 1920s, built by Maxim Motors of Middleboro, Massachusetts), joined the early fleet of fire engines at the Chesapeake City Volunteer Fire Co., No. 1.

dimensions for a new fire house at 30'x 20'x 18'. Mr. Harry Pensel drew up the plans. Mr. Brown was contracted, and he finished the building in November, 1911 for the sum of $800. When the canal was widened in the 1920s, the fire house was moved to the north side of town.

A new, larger, masonry fire hall was built in 1950. This same building was doubled in size in 1965 by Phillips Home Builders of Middletown, Delaware. The total cost of the 1965 addition was $35,000.

NEWS FLASH

"Marion Thompson, a senior of the High School, fractured a bone in his arm while cranking his car on Thursday afternoon."

– *Cecil County News,*
May 5, 1920

DID YOU KNOW?

The Chesapeake Basket Company in North Chesapeake City was destroyed by fire in 1906.

151

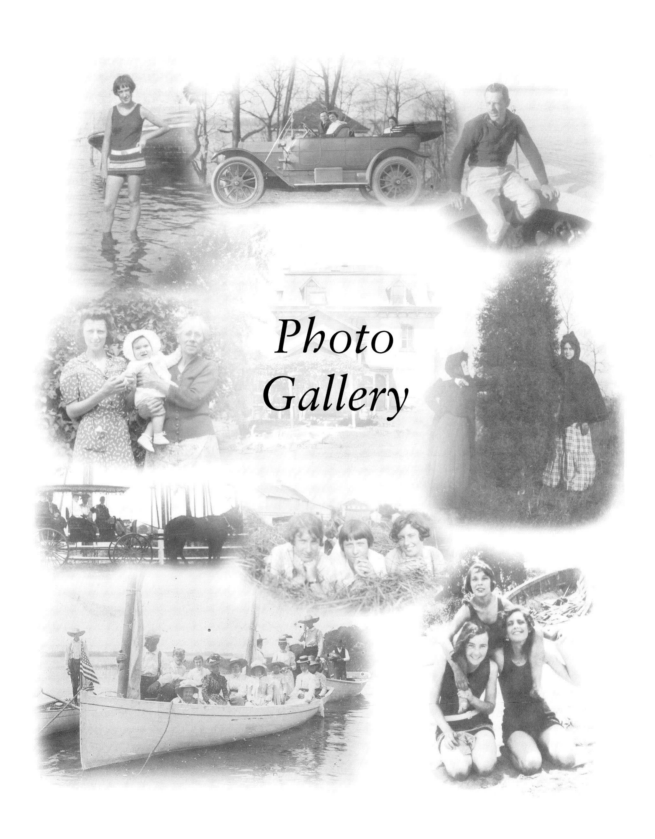

Photo Gallery

Circa 1910

Local waterman George Titter (right) is ready for a day's work on the bay. Fishermen and hunters often worked as hired captains aboard pleasure craft.

Two local bottles: A 1940's Losten's Dairy milk bottle (left), and a 1920's A. E. Hague soda bottle.

The entrance to the C & D Canal at the Chesapeake City lock, circa 1910. At left is the wharf area and the building which later housed Joseph Schaefer and Sons.

The Spa Springs Bottling Works of Chesapeake City, owned and operated by A. E. Hague in a building behind his residence on George Street, provided Chesapeake City and surrounding areas with soda. This soda crate is now on display at the Historical Society of Cecil County in Elkton, Maryland.

View north from the Lift Bridge, circa 1930. Schaefer's Market and the Ericsson Line Wharf are in the background.
..

Back Creek at Chesapeake City, circa 1921. Left to right: Schaefer's store and warehouses, lock entrance,

The waterfront at the end of Bohemia Avenue, circa 1930. The stern of the *Playhouse*, Adams' Floating Theatre, is on the left. Kibler's Ice House is in the center and the Harriott Hotel is on the right.

private home on the Causeway, and Masonic Hall. Dredges in the cofferdam are visible behind Schaefer's store.

Photos courtesy of Morrison Watson

The well-remembered 1942 collision of the vessel *Franz Klasen* with the Chesapeake City Lift Bridge is shown above. At left, the salvage team of Merritt, Chapman and Scott, of New York, removes the bridge's superstructure from the bow of the ship. Merritt, Chapman and Scott was the same company that removed the lock in the 1920s.

Schaefer's and the Mooring Basin, 1950

Photo courtesy of Roland "Flint" Sheldon

19th-Century Holiday Cards

North Chesapeake City, 1950

Photos courtesy of Roland "Flint" Sheldon

South Chesapeake City and Third Street, 1965

Photo courtesy of U.S. Army Corps of Engineers

View of Charles Street from Route 213 Bridge, circa 1950.

Route 213 Bridge and Schaefer's Market and Restaurant, circa 1950.

Welch Point

Elk River

C & D Canal

Southern Transportation

Boat Yard

North
Chesapeake City

South
Chesapeake City

Route 213 Bridge

Schaefer's

C & D Canal

Ferry Slip

Ferry Slip

Mooring Basin

U.S. Army
Corps of Engineers

Photo courtesy of U.S. Army Corps of Engineers

Chesapeake City and the Chesapeake and Delaware Canal, looking west, circa 1958.

Photo courtesy of Morrison Watson

Southern Transportation Co. on Long creek, right of center, circa 1940.

Harold Reynolds, Sr. on a small sailing skiff on Back Creek, circa 1900. The steam engine smokestack at the waterwheel complex is in the background.

The Chesapeake City Coronet Band of 1915. FRONT: Bill Toomey, Shorty Krastel, unknown, John Hudson. MIDDLE: unknown, unknown, unknown, Albert Ross, Ed Titter, unknown. BACK: Elmer Watson, Jay Sager, Frank Fillingame, Jacob Sager, unknown, George Norton Fillingame.

Port Herman Road, 1900

Photos courtesy of Mary Anna Taylor

ABOVE: Road to Port Herman, late nineteenth century.

LEFT: The first concession stand at Port Herman Beach, July 4, 1924.

Town Point Store and Post Office on
Port Herman Road.

1907

Port Herman Beach parking area, 1932.

1932

1900

Horse & buggy on Town Point Road.
Bohemia House is in the background.

BELOW: Same location today.

2000

1930s

This 1930s view of the basin on the south side of Chesapeake City shows the lift bridge connecting the north and south sides from George Street to Lock Street. Note the dredge tied at the government dock. Just above the roofline of the garage (foreground left), two large fuel storage tanks can be seen. Pure Oil distributed fuel to the residents and also fueled boats near the wharf area.

Photo courtesy of Lucy Titter

2000

Route 213 bridge spanning the canal at Chesapeake City. The basin is in the foreground.

A group of children and their toys (names and date unknown).

Yachts tied up in the mooring basin on the south side of Chesapeake City, circa 1930.

The Swing Farm at Town Point, circa 1900.

Town Point Wharf, circa 1900.

Biddle Street, looking west, circa 1945. Canal Street adjoins Biddle Street in the left foreground.

Mr. Hooven (right), a frequent visitor to Town Point from Philadelphia, poses with a fellow fisherman and a fresh catch of perch. Early 1920s.

Ruth Reynolds and Mr. Clarence Truss, 1930s.

LEFT: Schaefer's first launch, 1900.

BELOW: Helen Titter wading in the Bohemia River, 1920.

Agnes Titter   Curtis Titter

The presidential yacht *Williamsburg* navigates the canal with President Truman on board, circa 1948.

LEFT: Mr. Robert Donaldson at Bethel, Maryland, circa 1910.

BELOW: Ladies on Schaefer's Wharf near the entrance to the lock (background), circa 1915.

Photos courtesy of Morrison Watson

Canal Bridge, looking south, St. Georges, Del.

Mules lined up at St. George's Pivot Bridge, circa 1900.

GEORGE A. WOLF, WILMINGTON, DEL.

Postcard courtesy of Morrison Watson

River View House, Town Point, Md.

River View House, near Town Point, circa 1900.

Photo courtesy of Morrison Watson

Long Bridge and Bohemia Avenue, with the bugeye *Caradora* berthed at the wharf, circa 1890.

Photo courtesy of National Archives

The tug *Fortuna* tows the barges *Saranac* and *Biscayne*. *Saranac* was built by Deibert Brothers Shipyard in Elkton, Maryland and launched in 1913.

Thousands of brass spikes were used in the construction of the locks in the C & D Canal. This spike, over 7" in length, is from the Chesapeake City lock.

– from the collection of Morrison Watson

Photo courtesy of Morrison Watson

ABOVE: Morrison Watson on the water, with a stool of decoys stowed below.
LEFT: Ready for a day of duck hunting, with the curtains up on the bushwack boat.

A view of "Buck Bridge", showing the mule
tow path along the canal, circa 1915.

BACK CREEK

Lift Bridge

Long Bridge

Canal Lock

Lock Street

Steam Pump
and Waterwheel

Hemphill Street

Lewis Street

Biddle Street

CANAL

C & D Canal at
Chesapeake City,
circa 1927.

Curiosities

Diagram of C & D Canal Lock

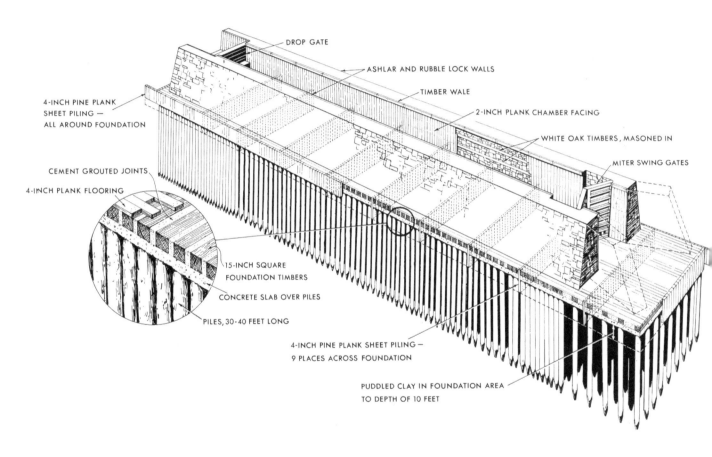

DROP GATE

ASHLAR AND RUBBLE LOCK WALLS

TIMBER WALE

2-INCH PLANK CHAMBER FACING

WHITE OAK TIMBERS, MASONED IN

MITER SWING GATES

4-INCH PINE PLANK
SHEET PILING —
ALL AROUND FOUNDATION

CEMENT GROUTED JOINTS

4-INCH PLANK FLOORING

15-INCH SQUARE
FOUNDATION TIMBERS

CONCRETE SLAB OVER PILES

PILES, 30-40 FEET LONG

4-INCH PINE PLANK SHEET PILING —
9 PLACES ACROSS FOUNDATION

PUDDLED CLAY IN FOUNDATION AREA
TO DEPTH OF 10 FEET

Courtesy of U.S. Army Corps of Engineers

Chesapeake and Delaware Canal Company.

INCORPORATED BY THE STATES OF PENNSYLVANIA, DELAWARE AND MARYLAND.

Mortgage Loan Scrip.

This is to Certify that the CHESAPEAKE AND DELAWARE CANAL COMPANY hereby acknowledges itself to be indebted to the registered owner hereof, or to the legal representative of such registered owner, in the sum of

_____ Dollars, lawful money of the United States of America (being part of the new loan authorized to be made at the meetings of the Stockholders and loan holders of the said Company held June 30th, 1855, under the provisions of the Acts of the Legislature of Maryland of May 25th, 1836, and of the Legislature of Delaware of June 15th, 1836, matured July 1st, 1886, and hereby agreed to be extended to July 1st, 1916, at the rate of interest and upon the security and conditions and convertible and redeemable as hereinafter expressed) which sum the said Company hereby promises to pay on the first day of July, A.D. 1916, with interest thereon at the rate of five per centum per annum, payable in like lawful money, semi-annually hereafter on the first days of the months of July and January, in each year, to such registered owner, or to the legal representative of such registered owner, at its office in the City of Philadelphia, State of Pennsylvania.

This Certificate is one of an issue of bonds or certificates of loan in even sums of $500 and $1,000 respectively, and in smaller odd sums, amounting in the whole to two million six hundred and two thousand nine hundred and fifty dollars, secured by a mortgage dated July 3d, 1855, of all the franchises, works, estate and property of the said Company, duly executed and delivered to Trustees and recorded in the offices for recording deeds, &c., at New Castle, in the State of Delaware, in Book P. Vol. 7, page 439, &c., and at Elkton, in the State of Maryland, in Liber W. H. R. No. 5, folio 301, &c., one of the Mortgage, &c., Record Books of Cecil County: this present issue being made in exchange for the previously existing and matured certificates of said loan, secured by the said mortgage, and in extension only and not in satisfaction of said loan, and upon the agreement that if the said mortgage shall be foreclosed or proceeded upon at the instance, or for the benefit of any holder of any of said matured certificates of said loan secured by said mortgage, the registered owner, or the legal representative of the registered owner hereof, shall be remitted to all the rights of the holder of the matured certificate exchanged for this certificate, as fully as if the said exchange and extension had not been made.

This Certificate is transferable by the registered owner, or the legal representative of the registered owner hereof, only in person or by an attorney duly authorized, upon the books of the Company at its office in the City of Philadelphia, or at any other place which it may designate, and a certificate of any such transfer is to be endorsed hereon. This Certificate is with other like certificates for odd sums convertible by the registered owner, or the legal representative of the registered owner hereof, into said bonds or certificates of loan for $500 and $1,000 respectively, in sums amounting thereto, at the option of the said Company, after five years from the date hereof. The interest on this Certificate shall cease at the maturity hereof, and satisfaction may be entered of record upon said mortgage in case this Certificate is not presented within two years after its maturity and the amount due thereon demanded and, in the event of refusal to pay, an action brought for the recovery of the same. This Certificate shall not become obligatory upon the said Chesapeake and Delaware Canal Company until the certificate endorsed hereon is signed by the trustee.

In Witness Whereof, The said Chesapeake and Delaware Canal Company has hereunto caused its common or corporate seal to be affixed hereto, duly attested, this _____ day of _____ A.D. 1887.

_____ President.

Attest

_____ Secretary.

SERIAL NUMBER
198919

ISSUE NUMBER
1–9

UNITED STATES
DEPARTMENT OF COMMERCE
BUREAU OF MARINE INSPECTION AND NAVIGATION

LICENSE TO CHIEF ENGINEER OF STEAM VESSELS

This is to certify that _Wilmer Bristow_ having been duly examined by the undersigned United States Local Inspectors, Bureau of Marine Inspection and Navigation, for the district of _Baltimore, Md._ as to his knowledge of steam machinery, and as to his experience, and found to be competent, is hereby licensed to act as Chief Engineer on _____ condensing _____ steam vessels of not over =1,000= gross tons, for the term of five years from this date.

Given under our hands this _22d_ day of _September, 1942._

Albert W. Schurgoll.
U.S. Local Inspector of Hulls. Merchant Marine Inspector in Charge.

U.S. Local Inspector of Boilers.

186

UNITED STATES DEPARTMENT OF COMMERCE
STEAMBOAT INSPECTION SERVICE

LICENSE TO FIRST-CLASS PILOT OF STEAM VESSELS

This is to certify that Benjamin F. Reynolds having given satisfactory evidence of the undersigned United States Local Inspectors Steamboat-Inspection Service, for the district of Baltimore Md., that he is trustworthy and faithful, and possesses the requisite knowledge and skill, is hereby licensed to act as First-Class Pilot on Steam Vessels of not over 700 gross tons, upon the waters of Chesapeake Bay & tributaries North & Patuxent River

for the term of five years from this date.

Given under our hands this 10th day of August, 192_.

Paul H. Tyler
U.S. Local Inspector of Hulls.

David C. Young
U.S. Local Inspector of Boilers.

| BACK OUR BOYS | # THE BRIDGE | BUY WAR STAMPS |

VOLUME 16 **Chesapeake City, Md., Nov . 30, 1944** **NUMBER 2**

Chesapeake School Aids Government in War Effort

This school, along with other schools all over America, has cooperated with the war effort by planning curricula which include features and subjects necessary for boys and girls going into the armed forces or into war-time jobs.

For example, the Army has found that most of the boys lacked knowledge of mathematics and English, and, as a result, mathematics, especially arithmetic, is being taught. In English, public speaking and journalism are being emphasized.

Other courses have also been changed with the war in mind. In history, modern and current subjects are stressed. The commercial course has been streamlined to prepare students to go into war-time jobs. The physical education program, to meet Uncle Sam's need for manpower, is stressing physical fitness

A new course, Global Geography, has been introduced to give studen   knowledge of   ɔbe and to prepar   ɔr ʰɛ post-   .ld.

.e cafet ʰ, vʰich   op-
..ated wit   Hor   ɪer,
and which pla. a ɡ   .on
Miss Crowgey, our c   .nd
the students who assist hei,   )en
mainly to see that, dui ɡ ti.,   ɪcy,
the nutritional needs .. the chil ɪ are
adequately met.

In cooperation with the government, stamps and bonds are sold regularly; travel has ᵇeen sharply curtailed, and the school, with the cooperation of the P. T. A., is attempting to provide clean entertainment that will keep the girls and boys off the street.

Local Boys Return From Foreign Duty

When Johnny comes marching home again, he finds the thrill of experiences, gained in far parts of the world with the Army and Navy, trifling compared with the thrill of just reaching home.

Even seeing the Pope could hardly compare with the excitement felt by Johnny Martin when he set foot in Chesapeake City. He had been in Italy about a year.

To Pete Dixon, his old bed was the most important thing. He had not slept in a bed for almost two years.

Other boys home from overseas are: Paul Nichols who has been gone for thirty-three months; Michael Harasymtzuk, who was previously stationed in England and is now confined to a hospital in New York; Francis Freet, who has served seventeen months in Italy and Africa and is now stationed in Philadelphia; Paul Luzetsky, serving in the United States Navy; Claude Beaston, who has been in two theatres of war and has been given a medical discharge; Woody Birch, who is in the United States Coast Guards, and has been serving overseas for about nine months; and William Cooling of the United States Navy, who was home for thirty days after being in action overseas.

The Honor Roll of Chesapeake City, dedicated Sunday, October 22, 1944

LOCAL HONOR ROLL SERVES AS SYMBOL TO COMMUNITY

The honor roll, which was dedicated on October 22, is a symbol of the courage and the bravery of the boys, whose names are recorded on it to the citizens of the town.

Interviews with citizens and students show a deep, tender feeling for this tribute to our boys which was made possible by the Civic Club.

Even the little children show a deep respect for it as they play along George Street where it stands, almost six feet from the ground, its gold eagle shining resplendently in the sun above its red, white, and blue colors.

Miss Katie Loveless whose energy and interest inspired the Civic Club to dedicate the honor roll, expresses the feeling of many of us when she says, "It is the finest way we know to show our appreciation for what the boys in the service are doing for us."

Mr. Nelson Cooling, whose son, Ned, is in the Navy, summed it up in this manner. "Our boys, especially those in foreign service, deserve the best that we can give them— anything for the boys. They are fighting to save our democracy and our form of government."

The name Luzetsky, which appears six times on the honor roll, represents the six sons of Alex Luzetsky and the brothers of Margaret Luzetsky, a Sophomore in Chesapeake City High School. Said Margaret, when asked how she felt about the honor roll, "I feel both proud and sad."

Dr. Henry V. Davis, whose home the honor roll faces, believes that the honor roll serves as a reminder to us at home, of the cost those who are taking full part in the war in many parts of the world are paying. He stated, "I believe that it is a good thing for us at home to be reminded in this way."

One hundred eleven of the two hundred sixty-two names listed on the honor roll are graduates of Chesapeake City High School, and practically all of the rest attended our school at some time or other. It is these men who have brought the full significance of war to our school and town.

Kelso

Kelso, with Milo Valenzuela up, winning the 1963 Gulfstream Park Handicap.

Kelso, one of the most storied thoroughbred race horses in history, was a product of Mrs. Richard C. duPont's Bohemia Stable. His notoriety brought fame to the little town of Chesapeake City. In thoroughbred racing circles, Kelso holds a most impressive record.

Kelso: *April 4, 1957 / Your Host -*
Maid of Flight
Owner: *Bohemia Stable*
Trainer: *C. H. Hanford*
Breeder: *Mrs. Richard C. duPont*
Jockeys: *Eddie Arcaro, Willie Shoemaker,*
Milo Valenzuela.

Kelso's Record Earnings

YEAR	Earnings
1959	$3,380
1960	$293,310
1961	$425,565
1962	$289,685
1963	$569,762
1964	$311,660
1965	$84,034
1966	$500
TOTAL	$1,977,896

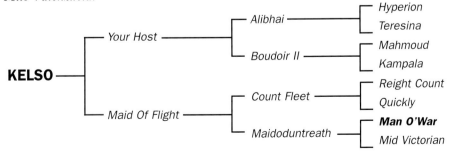

KELSO
— Your Host
— Alibhai
— Hyperion
— Teresina
— Boudoir II
— Mahmoud
— Kampala
— Maid Of Flight
— Count Fleet
— Reight Count
— Quickly
— Maidoduntreath
— **Man O'War**
— Mid Victorian

The Truss Murder Trial

Following is the newspaper report of a late 19th-century murder trial involving a Chesapeake City resident. Similar findings today might result in a ruling of insufficient evidence to convict the defendant. You be the judge:

Excerpts from the Cecil Whig, Saturday, March 28, 1896

HIS LIFE AT STAKE

James Henry Truss on Trial for the Murder of

CAPT. CAMP AT CHESAPEAKE CITY

Much Public Interest Shown – The Case One of Circumstantial Evidence and Tried Before Judge Wickes

The sun shone brightly through the courtroom on Tuesday morning when the trial of Truss began and the room was densely crowded, by a curious and deeply interested audience. Custodian Shockley did not open the public doors until five minutes before ten o'clock, when the witnesses began to arrive. The first important witnesses in the case were Mr. and Mrs. Irwin H. Deibert, Mr. Deibert being proprietor of the dry dock at Chesapeake City where Truss was employed and where the murder took place. Then, the doors a minute or two before ten o'clock were opened to the public, and the crowd surged in, the benches were filled to overflowing, and every available space was occupied. The main door to the left was the only one opened. Then Bailiff Harry Thomas arrived and the other door was opened.

Deputy Clerk of the Court John G. Williams was early at his place. The witnesses and talesman were directed to take places inside the rail. The whole county was interested in the case.

COURT OPENS

Judge Wickes convened court at a quarter to twelve o'clock.

Truss sat in one corner of the witness box, his sharp black eyes moving quickly from one part of the room to the other.

Judge Wickes instructed Clerk of the Court Williams to arraign the prisoner. Truss stood up during the reading of the indictment. His face bore an intent look. He leaned forward both hands resting on the rail of the prisoners box.

PLEA NOT GUILTY

In a firm and determined way Truss pleaded 'Not Guilty' and stated that he desired to be tried before the court.

"Gentlemen, the court is now ready to hear the case." said Judge Wickes.

Mr. Constable then had the prisoner brought to his side and he there remained during the trial.

Judge Wickes discharged the regular panel until 10 o'clock Thursday morning. The Talesmen on the murder case were finally discharged.

"I understand that it is your Honor's desire that we make a statement of the facts in this case for the information of the court." said Mr. Evans, State's Attorney, in opening the case. He then stated the circumstances appertaining to the murder of Captain Camp.

The circumstances in the case he said show that the murderer was acquainted with the dry dock and that he was acquainted with the movements and affairs of the victim.

The defense reserved its statement. Dr. Jos. V. Wallace, of Chesapeake City, practicing physician, was the first witness called by the state. He testified that he was in Chesapeake City and saw the body after it had been found on the afternoon after the day of the murder. The body when he saw it was lying in a shed, or outhouse on the dry dock. Did not make a close examination of the body, but looked over the grounds. A wallet was picked up before him, about eight feet away a pool of blood was found, along the river shore. The tide had wet part of the book. It was handed to Dr. Wallace by a certain Mr. Krastel and he looked into it, He found the address of a lady at Goshen, N. J., a lock of hair, a receipt, but he found no money in it. I again saw the body when and examination was conducted by the state on the following Saturday. A wound as large as a half dollar on back of the head, and fragments of the bone penetrated to and pressed upon the brain. There were several blows across the right side of the head. The brain was mashed to a pulp." Dr. Wallace thought any one of the wounds would have caused death. At the first blow a man would have been paralyzed. On the back of the head the wound could have been produced by the flat side of a sledge hammer and the wounds of the side with the rivet side. A hammer produced in the court found after the tragedy – Dr. Wallace was of the opinion could have been produced by the hammer.

CROSS EXAMINATION

Dr. Wallace said it was hard to tell exactly how many wounds there were.

Henry J. Pensel, a prominent merchant of Chesapeake City, testified that he knew Truss, who was a customer of his, buying dry goods and groceries. Had dealt with him up to October 12th last. Before that he had dealt with Pensel for four or five years. His bills averaged about $20, he having a pass-book which Mr. Pensel had at home. When he stopped, he owed Mr. Pensel $37.06. Truss was sent a bill and said he could not pay it then but could pay it later. In the latter part of the month, October 20th Truss said he had not been paid altogether by Mr. Deibert. Mr. Pensel found this to be untrue, and in December, about the tenth, he sent another 'due', and told him that part of his goods had been gotten under false pretenses. The bill is still unpaid.

He said by Truss's false pretenses, he meant the statement that Mr. Deibert had not paid him, which he understood to be untrue, as Mr. Deibert always paid his men. For the last one-half year Truss had averaged about $20 worth of goods a month. The last time that Truss paid him money was in September. In the matter of the average purchases Mr. Pensel was a little confused upon cross examination. The books were examined and the average monthly purchases were examined and found to be extensive. Truss wrote a note in reply to 'due' which Mr. Pensel had lost, his daughter destroying them. He promised to pay in December. But after Oct. 12 had no conversation – only correspondence, he receiving two notes from Truss. Pensel when he made the statement about false pretenses did not know personally whether Mr. Deibert had paid the men, and Truss, or not. Truss said he would pay Pensel interest on the bill if he would wait on him.

On re-direct testimony Pensel said that in the past six months Truss had gotten goods to the amount of $120.00.

Irwin Deibert, the owner of the dry dock at Chesapeake City, where Truss was employed and the scene of the murder, gave a plan of the grounds, was shown by a plat produced by the state. He stated that Truss was employed at the engine house. The engine house had a window of wood, like the weatherboarding.

In the engine house was a jar of coal oil on a shelf to the rear of the engine house, which a person unfamiliar with the building would be unable to find in the dark.

In passing from the boat of Captain Camp at the end of the dry dock, one would pass ten or twelve feet from the front of the engine house. The engine is 15 feet from the end of the dock. The engine house is 40 feet from the work shed.

The engine house door locked with hasp and pad lock with just a plain ordinary staple. The window was fastened inside with a hasp and a plug. On the outside you could see the hasp, there are cracks between the boards of the window. Truss was in my employ, but not on pay the day of the murder, nor the day before. I saw the Captain on Wednesday, I had one man at work that day – Wednesday. Saw Truss there and had a conversation that day with Captain Camp around the corner of the office. Truss was inside – the door was open. I didn't know what he was doing inside. When in the house it was possible for him to hear the conversation – there were places in the building where he could not have heard the conversation. When the conversation was over Truss came out. Truss's duty was to lock up the engine house. He had keys. Was not ordered to make fire in the engine house on Thursday evening.

On Wednesday, Jan. 2, I was in Elkton. On Thursday (day of murder) I was away. I was away part of the day on Jan. 1 and 2. During the time Truss had worked for me couldn't tell without his record book what I had paid him.

The State had instructed the witness to bring the record book, which he failed to do. They wanted the witness's testimony suspended until the book was produced. Mr. Constable objected.

Mr. Evans stated that the witness gave them to understand that he had the book and that he had been allowed to go on on the stand under those conditions as they thought.

Ex-State's attorney A. L. Crothers stated that the witness had informed him before going upon the stand that he had the book as he had been instructed to get it. "It appears to me that such a ruling would put the power in the hands of the witness to defeat the ends of justice." The state took every precaution.

Judge Wickes said the witness should have been examined more closely and that the prosecution should have been more positive on this point of law. He ruled that the examination of witness go on, and that the admissibility of the book would be determined when it was produced in court the next day.

Mr. Deibert then said that on Dec., 30th, he had paid Truss either $17 or $18. Paid him $1.85 a day. Never paid him $60 at any time. Never owed him more than one month at any pay day. Never let men wait longer than one or two or three days. Truss came to me six or seven weeks before the murder, to get me to endorse a note. First asked me to give him about $75. I said I hadn't the money to spare. This conversation took place in the evening. Then he said that Mr. Brady would give him the money, if I endorsed the note. He then came back next evening, with a $50 note signed. He said he wanted to buy a little house for $50, and it would require $25 to repair. On the second evening he said he had given up the idea of getting the house, and that out of the $50 note he wanted to pay Mr. Pensel, the merchant about $35.

Mr. Deibert did not endorse the note. I never told Truss not to go to the engine house without a pistol. Captain Camp's boat had been at the dock about 2 weeks for repairs. I saw Captain Camp have a note or two. Truss to his knowledge did not work any where except at the dock – he had charge of the buildings. He saw these notes he thought possibly a week before the murder.

CROSS EXAMINATION

Mr. Deibert had employed Truss as engineer and to take charge of the buildings for about sixteen months, ever since the works started.

There were two (2) keys to the engine house pad lock, I had one Truss had the other. Truss opened and locked the building. The door had been broken into twice before. The burglars stole the first time a pair of boots and a combination tool. The second robbery was not very long afterward, window was forced once, but nothing was taken. On the ground floor of the engine house there is a four inch pipe running across

the brick floor three-quarter inch above the floor. Captain Camp's boat was on the town side of the dry dock. The engine house door to dry dock is 20 feet, and from engine house to work shed 45 or 50 feet. It had been sometime that I had known of fire in engine house, a month. Was fire there on the Saturday after the murder. When the fire was made on Saturday, he noticed chunks of wood in the furnace partly burned, noticed them then – but his duties prevented him investigating the condition of the furnace very often. Didn't know how long the chunks had been there. The engine had not been run for a month. Left Chesapeake City on the Friday morning after seven o'clock and went to Philadelphia. Truss would often leave the engine house open to go to supper and then come back and lock up – and of which I complained.

About January 1st – I told the men that I expected to have work for them all winter. A person looking in the door could not see the jug. At the time of the murder work was slack at the dry dock. The engine house had tools in it, and was opened every time the men were at work.

J. K. P. Racine, of Elkton, had known the prisoner since his incarceration. Had several talks with him. He asked him after the preliminary hearing – "Well Truss how do you feel" – "Like an Innocent Man," said he. He said "what are the sentiments of the people." I said "that you are the guilty man." Truss said "How would it do for my sister to swear that I was saving money up to buy a bedroom suit." or something like that. I told him he would have to account for the money. I said you will have to get them to swear that you had this money. Truss said I expect my wife and sister up. He got Racine to mail a letter for him so the authorities wouldn't know of it, and Truss cautioned him not to say anything. When I came out Mackey asked me if I had mail from truss, and I gave him the letter. The first letter was to his wife – another was to Linda Savin, his sister. When I went to see him I had no idea that my testimony would be used in court.

EVENING SESSION

When Judge Wickes reconvened court at 6:15 J. Polk Racine was returned to the stand and Mr. Constable, Sr., again took up his cross examination. Racine said "before I went in Sheriff Mackey told me that if Truss gave me any mail for me to return it to him. I didn't understand him at first, I wasn't employed by the authorities to go there." When his condition was questioned, Racine stated that he was sober upon these occasions as stated. "No one requested me to question Truss. I knew a great murder had been committed."

Henry C. Hager, a grocer and provision dealer of Chesapeake City, had known Truss for several years. For two months prior to the murder he had been a customer. On the 28th or 30th of December he borrowed a half-dollar from me until pay day. He owed me the December store bill of $10.35. He paid it on the morning of the murder between 8 and 9 o'clock on Thursday, Jan. 2, also paid the borrowed money, it being included in the bill of $10.35. He borrowed the money in the evening between six and seven o'clock. Didn't say what he wanted it for. On cross examination by A. Constable, Jr., he said Truss's November bill was $12 and some cents. Was paid by him. Was not in my store the evening of the murder, Jan. 2. He was in the store about three o'clock on that day.

William Borger, a young boy of Chesapeake City, was at the home of Truss Sunday, Dec. 29th. Was in the house with Mrs. Truss, Harry Truss and Winfield Broadway. They were talking about some Epworth League badges. She showed me one and said I ought to get one. She said she wished Mr. Deibert would pay off soon as she wanted some boodle.

CROSS EXAMINATION

Truss had a hymn book and was looking over it. Truss certainly heard the conversation. Broadway had gone out then.

SHERIFF HARVEY H. MACKEY.

Sheriff Mackey knew Truss, having first seen him on the Saturday morning after the murder, when Truss was a member of the coroner's jury. He saw Truss on Sunday and Monday, he being arrested on Monday the evening. The letters spoken of by Racine, witness, were in the possession of Mr. Mackey, who had received them from Racine. Mr. Mackey then read the letters. They were addressed to Mrs. H. E. Truss and Mrs. Linda Savin, sister of the accused.

Feb. 3 1896

My Dear Loving Wife:–

I must see you if it lies in your power to do so. Pet, ask Linda if I did not tell her before Christmas I had money I had saved. Tell Linda to say I was in her house from 7 to 8:30. Look under the oil cloth in the hall and you will find some money.

Feb. 10 1896

Dear Linda:–

Wasn't I in your home on Jan. 2nd from 5:30 to 7:20. If you will see Mr. Constable and swear to it I will pay you $10 when I get out in March. You say I told you I had $75 saved up. I was mistaken about Deibert. Linda, when you see Albert Constable, he is my counselor, tell him about Deibert say you know I had money laid up and can swear to it. Linda, didn't I tell you before Christmas that I had money laid up for winter and would not break into it. Linda, say that I was in your house from 5:30 to 7:20 and there will be $10 for you when I get out in March

These letters were delivered to me and I read them. I then went to Chesapeake City, and Dr. Karsner and I went to the house, saw Mrs. Truss and made search of the house. Went into the hall, and raised up the oil cloth by the door. Found three ten dollar bills. Made a search of the premises the night of his arrest, Monday night – Jan. 6th. Found a purse containing $60 in the sewing machine drawer. Told Truss of it – he said it was money he had saved up and given to his wife on Friday, after the murder. Talked with Truss on the afternoon of his arrest in his yard, he was sawing wood. Seymour and I went there to question him in regard to breaking open of the engine house. He said he went to the engine house at seven o'clock and when he came around the corner of the shop on Friday morning, saw that the door had been broken out, and then he went into the office, and there talked with Peterson who was in there. Peterson said he thought Truss was in the engine house. Truss said he then went to the stable to feed the horse. Did not go first to the engine house, seeing that it had been forced open, although he had charge of it. Was with the horse three-quarters of an hour, and did some other things before he went to the engine house. Truss repented his statement about going to the engine house. This was about 7:30 in the evening that he had made this statement. To get him to the hotel Seymour and I went to his house and told him that the State's Attorney wanted to see him. First spoke to him about the burying of a dog some days before the murder. Truss had buried it with a long handled shovel, got no blood on him he said as he did not touch the dog. He had on the same shoes he said then that he buried the dog in. Had gloves on too, he said. The evening of the murder he said he had seen Captain Camp about 4:30 o'clock. He left the dock to go to the stable. Came back, locked the engine house and went to his house about ten minutes of six, and ate supper. Then sat down, read the paper. Stayed a while and at 7:30 went to the post office, at the time the last church bell ringing. Came back to the house about quarter to eight did not go out again. Afternoon day of arrest – made an investigation around the engine house. Back of the fly wheel I found a pair of rubber boots. They seemed to have been wet recently, as on the inside they were frozen.

Rained a little on Friday and blew up very cold, freezing weather. Monday was very cold. The boots had mud on them, and something that I took to be blood. Where the body was found – engine house door to edge – hard and gravely, but along the water being soft, and one gets mud on their boots going there. The tide made the mud. Also found clothing, on the driver of the engine was an old blouse, saturated with what I though to be lubricating oil. Back of the boiler was found a pair of old pants. They were shown to Truss at the hotel. First the boots. Truss said the first boot was not his. The second boot he said was his. Afterward he admitted that they were his. When talking of boots at first he said his boot had a hole in it – the first one did not, but a hole was in the second one – and he acknowledged its ownership. He said his boots were back of the fly wheel of the engine where we found them. I searched him. He had in money $3.52 beside two old coins. He said nothing then of the money at the house. Then something was said of searching the house. He then said he had always saved money – but did not mention having money until the searching of the house was brought up. Found clothing at the house, one article being a shirt he had worn on the day of the murder – a pair of blue overalls and three blouses. The shirt was a light one. There was a stain on the breast of the shirt which I took to be blood. A place was cut out of one of the sleeves. A cane was picked up in the engine house. A shovel was found on Saturday, I was not present at the time. On the handle of the shovel appeared blood and mud marks. A hand seemed to be imprinted on the handle, stains showing marks of a hand from which parts were gone. I did not find the shovel. The impression of the hand was only a portion. The marks on the handle are not as clear now as they were, said Sheriff Mackey when the shovel was exhibited to the court. Sheriff Mackey said that one of the hands of Truss was short of three fingers. Sheriff Mackey did not feel able to say whether the hands of Truss could have made the marks. Truss held up his right hand and which had only the index finger.

Truss said that when he went to the shop the sledge hammer was lying in the door the handle lying partly out. He said he set it back where it belonged. Truss said on the coroner's jury several times that some people around there were trying to get his position. When you think so why do you not say who you suspect of breaking into the shop? Said he thought but it didn't do to think too loud. He seemed to think that the parties that broke into the house had committed the murder. After his arrest he spoke of his innocence. Truss stated that he thought some enemy of his had done it. I think it was Harry Vance and Andy Spittle he suspected. On Wednesday he sent for me in jail. He said go and arrest Jim Moore and you will have the man. I said I would send the State's Attorney, and that official did go and get Truss's statement. A large grip containing boots and other articles of clothing were shown, as above mentioned. I took the boots to Dr. Wormley, of Philadelphia, and had them examined. Also took shirt and sledge and other articles of clothing. At or very close to engine house I found what looked like blood, it trailed to a point back of work shed where there was a pool of blood, and off toward the water was another smaller pool. The face of the corpse was scratched indicating that the body had been dragged. Among the articles taken from Truss was the promissory note to Deibert.

WM. S. EVANS, STATES ATTORNEY

The present State's Attorney W. S. Evans next took the stand, and testified. Mr. Crothers started the inquiry. Mr. Evans was at the inquest and went with Mr. Crothers to Chesapeake City on the Monday evening following and at Queck's hotel met Seymour Mackey and Banks. The shovel, sledge and bar of iron were there in Mackey's charge. Nothing had as yet been developed, though Truss was suspected. He was sent for and examined. Evans took notes of Truss' replies who knew that he was being examined. Mr. Evans read the statement which confirmed and amplified Sheriff Mackey's testimony as stated above.

DR. WORMLEY

Prof. Wormley who holds the chair of chemistry and toxicology in the University of Pennsylvania examined chemically and microscopically the blood stains on the shirt, blouse, hammer and gum boots. The stains gave me results either blood crystals or blood corpuscles the diameters of which showed that the blood was that of a limited class of mammals, which included man, monkeys, kangaroos, seals and the opossum. Prof. Woodward alone of the experts held that the diameters of human and dog blood corpuscles were practically the same.

MRS. SLUYTER BOUCHELL

Mrs. Sluyter Bouchell, of Chesapeake City, saw sparks and smoke coming out of the dry dock smokestack after supper on the night of the murder. Her son, Elmer, and Edward Eddison, colored, also saw the smoke.

JOHN MILLER

John Miller, a merchant of Chesapeake City testified that Truss rented a house from him at $4 a month, and paid by the quarter. Truss came to Miller's store between 7:40 and 8 p.m. on January 2, the day after the murder, and paid $12 for the September quarter still owing the December quarter. He gave Miller a $10 and $5 note and got $3 change. He then bought 65 cents worth of goods. Truss said he would pay the next quarters rent the first of February, as he was a little short of money. His appearance was as usual. He was there about half an hour, was not at all excited, and went to the post office, and returning got his goods. Truss was dressed in his working clothes as near as he could recall.

MRS. LINDA SAVIN

Mrs. Linda Savin, sister of Truss lives on George Street, Chesapeake City. Truss lives on Charles Street, the next south. Truss did not tell her in December or at any other time that he had money saved up. Could not say but did not think that Truss was at her house on the night of the murder, nor was he there that afternoon. To the defense: Truss would often spend the evenings at her house some weeks four or five evenings. He only lived about a square away. Would come about 5:30 or 6 and stay perhaps until 7 or later. As to New Year's week could not recall how often he was at her house. Could not say whether he was there on the night of January 2. Could not recall that she said Truss was at her house on the evening of the murder. Would be glad to say so if she could. Could not recall that Truss told her that he had to go to the post office to get a money order or that he gave her a postal card.

CAPT. CAMP'S DAUGHTER

He had the check cashed in Salem on December 14. We left Salem and came to Chesapeake City, reaching there on December 17. The boat was taken to Deibert's dry dock for some repairs. The expense going through he canal was but $0.25. The crew on the boat, two colored men, left us at Salem. I left Chesapeake City on December 23, about 10 o'clock. Father had money with him and gave me $5 before I went. He then described the kind of pocket book and its color. I saw the pocketbook again after the murder. He had more than one hundred dollars when I left him at Chesapeake City. I was on the boat Sunday after the murder and saw the potatoes on the stove in a quart cup. They were scorched. Father had two revolvers – one a British bull-dog self cocker. He kept the revolver under the lounge in the cabin, which was the same room the stove was in. It was missing after the murder and I could not find it, although I searched for it in the presence of my cousin and others. That was on Sunday, and on Monday I searched again and found it under the lounge. The door to the cabin was not locked and anyone could have gotten into the room. I received a letter from my father dated December 31st, in which he requested me to come to Chesapeake City as the Manaway was about to make a trip. Had I gone, I would have arrived at Chesapeake City on January 2, the night of the murder. I replied to his letter but he never received it. Father had his life insured for $155. He was a quiet man, and never had any trouble with him nor with his crew. The testimony of young Camp was important, in view of the fact that it now proves without a doubt that Camp was in possession of a large sum of money on the night of the murder.

MRS. DEIBERT'S TESTIMONY

Mrs. Irwin Deibert, wife of the owner of the dry dock, was an important witness. Her testimony was that on the morning after the murder she was up by 5:30 and about 7 o'clock Truss came along and told her the engine house had been broken into the last night and said that a half gallon of oil had spilled over the floor and the can was mashed to pieces. He said there was nothing taken. "I learned of the murder about 8 o'clock, when I and my little boy were taking a walk down toward the dry dock. My little boy called my attention to an object in the water and I soon discovered it was the body of a man. I suppose he had been drowned. I told George Peterson about my discovery, and he said that is the man I have been looking for all day. Truss soon came down and I said "Ain't it awful about the man being drowned" and he replied, 'Yes it is.' Truss did not go to see the body, but remained in the engine house until called out by Peterson, who was employed at the dock as a carpenter. I asked Truss what would be done with the body, and he replied that Mr. Coleman, the undertaker, would attend to it. I said something about bringing it into the engine room and he said "No sir, I don't want it put in there, as I have a dread of dead people."

MRS. LIZZY BUCKWITH

Mrs. Lizzie Buckwith, of Chesapeake City, testified that Mrs. James Truss was at her house on the night of January 2, the night of the murder. They lived close together. Mrs. Truss came into the house about 6:30 and remained until 8 or 9 o'clock. Mr. Truss called her. He came up to the gate and called her very loudly, saying, "Rach, Rach." His manner indicated that he was in a hurry. I remarked to Mrs. Truss at the time. "My Lord, Rach, what is the matter with Harry." Did not see Truss again until at the dry dock. I had a conversation with him about the pistol. He was in my house on Monday. He said they had their suspicion who did it, also said on Thursday night there was a tall yellow man standing on the corner and he said to a woman and child going to the boat 'how many officers are there in this town?" The woman said three. The man said there would be someone suffer in town before morning. Monday afternoon Mrs. Truss said to Mr. Truss that if they had a watchman last night they would have caught the man as the pistol he had taken back to the boat and laid on the table.

WINFIELD BROADWAY

Winfield Broadway testified that he was a brother-in-law of Truss and boarded with him. He said he found a cane, which looked like the one found in the engine room, and had taken it and thrown it on Truss's woodpile in the summer. He said he could not state for sure if it was the same cane, but looked like it. "I was at Truss' house on the night of the murder and ate my supper about 5 o'clock. Truss and his wife and myself sat down together. Truss was the first to get through, and he went out and I did not see him any more that night. I was with Sheriff Mackey when he found the $60 in the sewing machine drawer."

ALDRICH GIBBS

Aldrich Gibbs, colored, testified that he found on Friday afternoon a ring of keys, on Front Street between George and Charles Streets, not far from an alley which runs past the home of Truss. The evidence was to prove that if Truss had committed the murder he went out of his way to reach home, and could have lost the keys where they were found.

DR. KARSNER

Dr. William C. Karsner testified to the wounds on the head of the victim.

JOHN METZ

John Metz, said Truss was used to handling sledges as he had often helped him at blacksmithing.

GEORGE W. PETERSON

George Peterson, carpenter at the dry dock repeated in the main, his testimony at the hearing. He got to the dock shortly before 7 o'clock and saw the engine house door and window open. Thought Truss was about and called, climbed in the window of the office and made a fire. Truss came in about ten minutes and opened the door. Asked Peterson if he had opened the engine house. Truss went out and came back in three or four minutes and said nothing was missing. Truss left shortly after to feed Deibert's horse. Truss came back painted a wagon brown, washed a carriage, and was around at different times during the day. Peterson was working on Camp's boat and needed him toward noon and felt worried at not seeing him. Saw him last about 4 p.m. the day before. Truss left before Peterson did on the 2nd, but probably came back to close up as that was his practice. Towards 3 o'clock on the 3rd, Mrs. Deibert called him to the dock to see a drowned man whom she and her little boy saw there. Saw Truss in his yard and told him that the man was drowned and he (Peterson) thought it was Camp. Truss and Mrs. Deibert were in the office when he came back. He thought Truss helped to carry Camp's body into the engine room. Did not hear him object to bringing the body there. The foreman of the jury had it moved to the office. Peterson described the fastening of the door. The shutter or shutter-window which fastened inside was shown in the court. Court then adjourned until Friday.

FRIDAY

Peterson recalled Truss to get his tools off the boat. Found them in the office or shop when he returned from Vandergrift's.

George H. Queck was to have shown the hasp of the engine house door but lost it on the way up. One shown him in court was just like it but smaller. It was a folding hasp fitting a plate staple which was put on with nails. The staple had been drawn out but the hasp was not twisted nor cracked.

C. D. Strickland testified that Chesapeake letters for North East, left Elkton at 8:28 a.m. and 5:16 p.m.

Lynch recalled. Could not say whether he came to Elkton on Jan. 3rd, on the 8 or 11 o'clock train from North East. If on the former could not have gotten Mrs. Truss's letter, if it was then at North East. Got it after 5 p.m. that day. The State here closed.

For the defense. Winfield Broadway recollected Albert Constable, Jr., asking Mrs. Savin about Truss being at her house on Jan 2nd, at night. She said she could not say yes or no. Mr. Constable confirmed this but told of her telling him on seeing her again that she had recollected it just after he had left her. She gave some details of his stay at her home that evening which was from about 6 to 7:30 p.m.

Bennett Savin, 8 years old thought his uncle

Harry was at his mother's the night before the dead man was found at the dock. Knew his mother was folding clothes but could not tell anything that was said or done by Truss, nor could he recall that Truss was there the next night or any other one night, though he often came there of evenings and stayed some time. The defense closed here and argument was begun at 5 minutes of 12 o'clock, Mr. Evans opening for the State.

TRUSS GUILTY

OF THE MURDER OF CAPTAIN CAMP AT CHESAPEAKE CITY

The Prisoner Bears Up Well When The Verdict of the Court is Pronounced

Judge Joseph E. Wickes, before whom the trial of James Harry Truss, who was indicted for the murder of Captain Thomas Camp, at Chesapeake City, was tried, last week, delivered the opinion of the court on Tuesday afternoon, at half past two o'clock when the prisoner was pronounced "Guilty of Murder in the First Degree".

Judge Wickes in his charge carefully went over the circumstances in the case which had led to his opinion – and by his exhaustive review of it at once gave evidence that the Court had arrived at such a conclusion only after a judicious and impartial consideration in which absolute fairness had been shown the prisoner.

In delivering his decision Judge Wickes said in part:– I am now prepared to render the verdict of this court in the case of J. Harry Truss, indicted for the murder of Thomas Camp. In this case the prisoner waived a trial by jury and selected the Court.

This case has placed a great responsibility upon me. On the one hand I must consider the life of the prisoner – on the other the safety and peace of society. It is a case of circumstantial evidence. No one saw the deed committed. It is the settled law in such cases: First - That the facts and circumstances from which guilt is to be inferred should be proved beyond a reasonable doubt. Second- The party charged is presumed to be innocent, until the contrary appears, and that presumption of innocence must contribute as one of the elements of proof to produce that condition of mind called reasonable doubt. Third - the facts proved must not only be consistent with the prisoner's guilt but must be inconsistent with every other

rational conclusion. These are the rules by which I have been guided in this case, and which I have applied to the best of my ability, to the testimony.

I do not deem it necessary to examine in detail the testimony in the case. There was much evidence and the case was elaborately and fully argued, and I shall only state my conclusions upon the several facts and circumstances upon which the State relies to prove the guilt of the prisoner.

It was conclusively shown that the prisoner knew Captain Camp and by his own statement saw him several times on Thursday afternoon. He also knew that Camp expected a friend by the midnight boat that night. It was clearly shown that the prisoner left the dry dock a few minutes before 5 o'clock – that he got his supper a few minutes after 5, and left his home immediately. I am satisfied that he returned at once to the dry dock reaching it between half past five and six o'clock. That he made a fire in the engine house although it was a mild night, remained there until nearly eight o'clock, and was next seen at Mrs. Buckwith's calling his wife and paying a bill to Mr. Miller, a merchant. Between the hours of half past five and half past seven Camp was murdered.

The engine house was found broken open Friday morning before the prisoner returned to the dry dock. I am satisfied that the prisoner returned to the dry dock. I am satisfied that the prisoner broke it open the evening before, although he had the key and left the sledge hammer, shovel and old blouse and gum boots with blood on them, to direct suspicion from himself and make it appear that some other person had committed the deed.

The stains on the hammer, shovel and blouse, and on the prisoner's shirt found at his house, were proved by Dr. Wormley to be bloodstains. The impressions in the mud on the handle of the spade were such as the prisoner's hand would make, having but a thumb and index finger, and the stumps of two other fingers.

The prisoner informed Henry Jones and Mrs. Deibert on Friday morning before he had gone to the dry dock that the engine house had been broken open.

It is also clearly proved that the prisoner was in debt and pressed for money, that he had not paid any rent since June and other creditors were making demands upon him. And he had been suspended from the society to which he belonged for arrears of dues. Immediately after the murder – beginning Thursday night about 8 o'clock he began to pay his debts. There was found in the possession of his wife $60, and secreted under the oil cloth $30. Friday morning he sent the money order for $7.50 to the witness Lynch, paid Henry Miller $12. The amount of money the prisoner had in his possession with the amounts paid to creditors within 24 hours after the murder corresponded with the amount proved to have been in Captain Camp's possession.

Although arrested the fourth day after the murder he was unable to show where he was between 5:30 and 8 o'clock Thursday evening. First he said that after fastening up the engine house he returned home at once and spent the evening there. Failing in this at the hearing before the Justice of the Peace, he then wrote letters to his wife and sister which were then intercepted by the Sheriff, urging his sister to swear that he was at her house from half past 5 to 7:30, and saying that he would give her $10 when he returned. This she refused to do but testified at the trial that he was not there. Nor do I suppose for one second that he was in her house that evening. In those letters he tells his wife of the money secreted under the oil cloth.

TRUSS SENTENCED

He Hears His Doom Unmoved

It being generally understood, that upon the assembling of court on Saturday morning, James Henry Truss, convicted of the murder of Captain Thomas Camp would receive his death sentence, the court room was filled with a curious and interested crowd of persons from nearly all sections of the county, a large number of persons from Chesapeake City and vicinity being present.

At ten o'clock, court was called with Judges Russum Stump and Wickes on the Bench. A few minutes after the Judges had taken their seats, the condemned man was brought into the court room with Sheriff Mackey and seated in the dock.

Judge Wickes before whom Truss had been tried, turning to the prisoner said:

"James Henry Truss, you have been convicted of the willful murder of Thomas Camp. Have you anything to say why sentence of death should not be pronounced upon you according to law?"

Truss still remaining in his seat and without visible emotion replied: "Yes, I have this to say, that you did not give me justice."

"What is that?" said Judge Wickes.

"You did not give me justice," again replied Truss.

"Have you anything else to say?" said the Judge.

To this inquiry, Truss sullen and morose made no reply, when Judge Wickes, with visible emotion, and evidently more sensible of the impressiveness of the occasion than the prisoner, continued:

"No one can fail to feel pity for you in your extremity but all who heard the testimony and are familiar with the facts of the case must feel that your fate is deserved. You have committed a terrible crime and merit the extreme penalty of the law. You waived your right to a trial by jury and elected to be tried before the Court, I knew nothing of the case when the trial began except that a man named Camp had been murdered at Chesapeake City, and that you had been suspected. I had not read the reports of the hearing before the magistrate and did not know the basis of the State's case. Your counsel did all they could for your benefit, and I listened to elaborate arguments in your behalf. I gave careful and long consideration to the testimony and arguments to find something in your favor, but could find nothing. I then had and now have no doubt of your guilt. You were in need of money and for a man of your means, were very much in debt. After Camp's murder an amount of money was found in your house corresponding very nearly with a sum which he was shown to have had about him. You did not show where you were that fateful evening. You tried to get your sister to swear that you spent it at her house. You did not seek to explain the blood stains on your garments or the marks on the sledge and shovel handle. Your life is forfeited. All that remains for you now is to seek the forgiveness of God.

The sentence of the Court is that you be removed hence to the jail of Cecil County and be there confined till the day fixed for your execution, when you shall be taken to the place of execution and there be hanged by the neck until you are dead. And may God, in His infinite goodness, have mercy on your soul."

Throughout the entire imposition of the sentence, Truss preserved the same self-contained and rigid manner he has worn throughout the trial. Apparently he had perfect self control. Not a muscle moved, while he looked intently at Judge Wickes, his small piercing eyes being fixed, and determined, the only indication of feeling on his part, being a shade pallor which passed over his face as he made his short and curt replies to the Court.

After receiving his sentence, Truss was taken from the court room by direction of the Court, and in the custody of Sheriff Mackey returned to the county jail.

TRUSS' LAST HOUR

The condemned passed his last night on earth quietly, although his sleep was not sound. Deputy Sheriff McAllister kept the last night watch. The Rev. Mr. Westerfield remained with him until 9 o'clock and engaged in religious conversation with him. The undertaker also called and Truss talked over his funeral arrangements. Truss desired that his body be taken to his home in Chesapeake City and services held on Monday, it also being his wish that his body be buried in Bethel Cemetery.

About 11:00, he stretched out and was soon in light slumber. He did not arise on the morning of his execution until about 6 o'clock, and when asked by the watch how he had rested and felt, replied brightly that he had rested first rate and felt well. Shortly after 7 o'clock he ate a hearty breakfast, consisting of ham and eggs, potatoes, bread and coffee. After breakfast, he dressed for his execution, putting on a new black sack coat, which had been secured for him by Sheriff Mackey, also a laundered shirt, with turn-down collar and black bow necktie.

At 10 o'clock the Rev. Mr. Westerfield entered the condemned man's cell, and was later joined by Rev. Mr. Mowbray, who remained with him to the last. The ministers offered him every religious consolation, sang and talked with him, and read passages from the scriptures. Truss remained quiet and attentive, and when asked if he appreciated his position said that he did, and when urged to make a confession in case of his guilt and go before his Maker prepared, he in a solemn manner stated that he had no knowledge of the crime and was entirely innocent, and that he was a Christian man and felt that he was saved. When prayer was offered he knelt down. Throughout the service Truss seemed reflective, but remained unmoved, and did not join in the singing.

All being in readiness Sheriff Mackey and Deputy McAllister entered the cell at 12:35. The condemned man's hands were handcuffed in front of him. He stood the trying ordeal without tremor, and when the march to the scaffold was begun he walked with a firm step. Sheriff Mackey and Deputy McAllister were on either side of him while the ministers walked in front.

As they passed down the iron staircase from his cell and the upper tier, through the jail corridor and out into the yard to the scaffold, Truss never flinched, but kept his eyes fixed downward in front of him. He did not look around when they had taken their places upon the scaffold.

Mr. Westerfield began the service by reading a portion of the 139th Psalm, after which Mr. Mowbray offered prayer. A part of the burial service was read by Mr. Westerfield, when the ministers shook hands with him and bade him good bye, leaving the scaffold. Truss' nerve was remarkable and he stood firm when the straps were adjusted to his arms and legs. There was hardly a movement upon his features, except a slight flush that passed over his face after the noose had been adjusted, and when the black cap was being drawn on. He was then placed in position on the trap, when Sheriff Mackey cut the rope with a hatchet, allowing the trap to drop. Every part of the machinery worked perfectly.

CECIL WHIG, June 27, 1896

TRUSS HANGED

The Murderer of Captain Thomas Camp

MEETS HIS DEATH CALMLY

Protested His Innocence of the
Crime to The End. His Death Painless

James Henry Truss, the murderer of Captain Thomas Camp, was hanged in the Elkton Jail yard at seventeen minutes of one o'clock yesterday, Friday afternoon. Nineteen minutes after the drop fell he was pronounced dead, and the body was cut down. Death resulted from strangulation and shock, but he suffered no pain, being rendered unconscious by the fall.

The condemned man protested his innocence to the end and met his death calmly and with no show of fear. The execution in every way passed off smoothly and successfully, and with the exception of several muscular contortions the body remained motionless after the fall.

The execution was witnessed by about forty people, among those present being Frank Camp, son of Captain Thomas Camp, the victim, and Winfield Broadway, of Chesapeake City. brother-in-law of the murderer.

The body was placed in a stained walnut casket and buried on the Alms House property at Cherry Hill, by undertaker Henry Vinsinger, of Elkton, with whom Truss had made all the arrangements. It was his desire that he should be buried in the Bethel Cemetery, but this could not be done.

Dr. John H. Jamar, the jail physician, was in attendance and made the examination pronouncing the man dead.

COME
AGAIN

"New children play upon the green,
New weary sleep below;
And still the pensive spring returns,
And still the punctual snow."

– Emily Dickenson

Acknowledgements

Contributors

Frank & Ida Briscoe

Frank was born in 1909 on the Briscoe Farm at Town Point. He married Ida Schrader of Summit, Delaware on Easter Sunday, 1931. They farmed, while raising their family, until the mid-1950s when Frank went to work for the Corps of Engineers in Chesapeake City. Now retired, he and Ida reside in lower Delaware, where they remain active in their church.

Bill & Margaret Briscoe

Born in 1916 on a Town Point farm, Bill (brother to Frank, top photo) resides in Galena, Maryland with his wife, Margaret. Bill spent his early years in and around Chesapeake City. He worked in Galena for Woodall and Stidham until his retirement. He remembers well Chesapeake City in the 1920s and '30s.

Eloise H. Davis

Eloise Howard Davis was born in 1913 at Randalia, near Chesapeake City. She married Chespeake City doctor Henry V. Davis in 1937. They raised a family and retired to Randalia. Eloise is a member of D.A.R. and has always been interested in local history.

Allaire C. duPont

Mrs. duPont moved to the Chesapeake City area just after WW II. She and her late husband raised and trained thoroughbred horses, including racing legend Kelso, on Woodstock Farm. Mrs. duPont has an avid interest in the preservation of Chesapeake City and the rural areas surrounding the town. She resides on her farm near St. Augustine.

Ralph & Anna Pyle

Ralph was born in 1910 on a farm on Court House Point Road, near Chesapeake City, Anna was born in 1913 on a farm at Witt's Corner, in Grove Point neck. They farmed in the Chesapeake City area until their retirement. Ralph's interests include caning, carving, and gardening. "Miss Anna" was the local high school principals' secretary for many years.

John & Bertha Sager

John is a third-generation Chesapeake City native. Born in 1913, he married Bertha Jackson of Elk Mills in 1937. They have lived in Chesapeake City all their married life. John retired from Amoco and Bertha from the Board of Education in 1978. They have five grandchildren and five great-grandchildren. The Sagers have had a life-long interest in the town of Chesapeake City, and are authorities on its history.

Dick & Janet Titter

Dick and Janet, married in 1991, were both born and raised in Chesapeake City area. They both raised families and worked in Chesapeake City. Now retired, Dick operated his own service station business for 35 years, and was a waterman in his early years. Janet is retired from County Bank. They reside near Chesapeake City.

Lucy F. Titter

Lucy has always lived in and around Chesapeake City. She and her late husband, Jack, raised their family while working in the family service station business and the local fishing market. Lucy has been a life-long member and supporter of Trinity Methodist Church, in Chesapeake City. She enjoys sharing her memories and photos of Chesapeake City in the old days.

Morrison Watson

Morrison was born in Bethel in 1918 and moved to Chesapeake City at the age of 10. He worked as a plumber until his retirement in 1980. Widowed in 1987, he resided in the same house from 1938 until his death, February 2001. He is buried at Bethel Cemetery. Morrison was a local authority on the canal and the town of Chesapeake City.

Additional Contributors

For personal recollections, documents,
and/or photographs, we also thank

Rose Marie Hall Austin

Lee Collins

Walter Cooling

Henrietta R. Crawford

Lisa Doricchi

Virginia R. Kerslake

Ed Losten

Debbie Lovejoy

Eleanor Lucas

Margaret Morgan

Arthur Raisin

Harold Reynolds

Earl and Anna Schrader

Lois Sewell

Roland "Flint" Sheldon

Mary Anna Taylor

John Trush

Mary Jackson Watson

Sources

The National Waterway – A History of the Chesapeake and Delaware Canal 1769-1985 by Ralph D. Gray. University of Illinois Press. 1967.

This Was Chesapeake Bay by Robert H. Burgess. Cornell Maritime Press, Cambridge, Maryland. 1963.

The District – A History of the Philadelphia District U. S. Army Corps of Engineers • 1866-1971 by Frank E. Snyder and Brian H. Guss. U. S. Army Corps of Engineers, Philadelphia, Pennsylvania. January, 1974.

The Old Bay Line, 1840-1940 by Alexander Crosby Brown. Bonanza Books, New York, N.Y. 1940.

Ukranians of Maryland by Basarob, Fenchak, and Wolodymyr. Ukranian Education Association of Maryland, Baltimore, Maryland. 1977.

History of Cecil County by George Johnston. Genealogical Publishing Co., Inc., Elkton, Maryland. 1881. Reprinted by Regional Publishing Co., Baltimore, Maryland. 1989.

Champlain to Chesapeake – A Canal Era Pictorial Cruise by William J. McKelvey, Jr. Canal Press, Inc. Exton, Pennsylvania. 1978.

At the Head of the Bay by The Cecil Historical Trust. The Maryland Historical Trust Press, Crownsville, Maryland. 1996.

The Outlaw Gunner by Harry M. Walsh. Tidewater Publishers, Centerville, Maryland. 1971.

The Chesapeake and Delaware Canal: Gateway To Paradise by Edward J. Ludwig, III. Cecil County Bicentennial Committee, Elkton, Maryland. 1979.

Decoys of the Susquehanna Flats and Their Makers by J. Evans McKinney. The Holly Press, Hockessin, Delaware. 1978.

The Cecil Whig, Elkton, Maryland.

The Historical Society of Cecil County, Elkton, Maryland.

Volunteer Fire Company No. 1 of Chesapeake City

U. S. Army Corps of Engineers, Philadelphia District, Chesapeake City, Maryland.

C & D Canal Museum, Chesapeake City, Maryland.

National Archives and Records Adminsitration, Still Photos Division, College Park, Maryland.

Chesapeake City, Maryland – 200

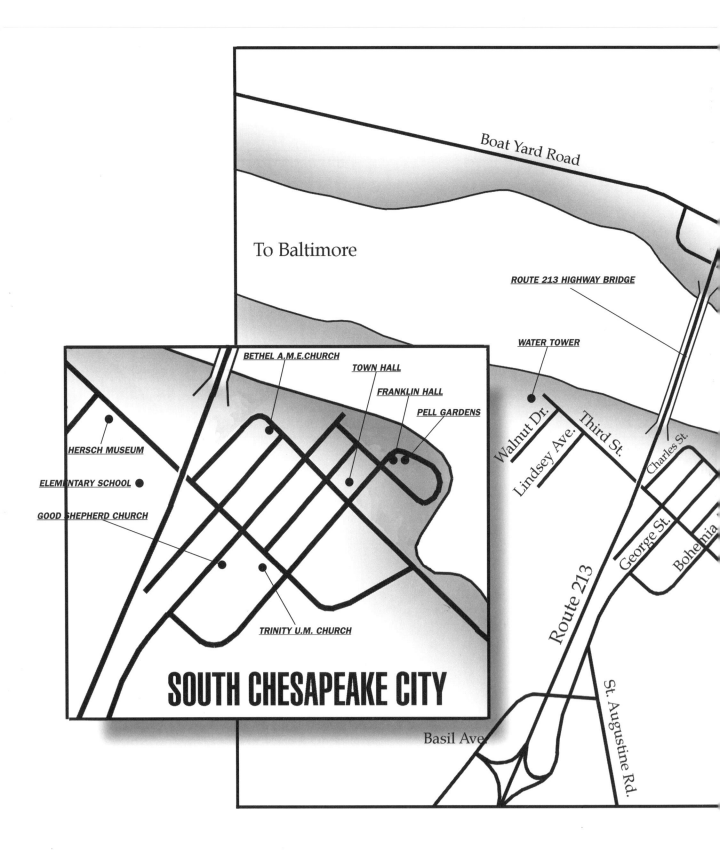

Boat Yard Road

To Baltimore

ROUTE 213 HIGHWAY BRIDGE

WATER TOWER

BETHEL A.M.E.CHURCH

TOWN HALL

FRANKLIN HALL

PELL GARDENS

HERSCH MUSEUM

ELEMENTARY SCHOOL

GOOD SHEPHERD CHURCH

TRINITY U.M. CHURCH

SOUTH CHESAPEAKE CITY

Walnut Dr.

Lindsey Ave.

Third St.

Charles St.

Route 213

George St.

Bohemia

Basil Ave.

St. Augustine Rd.